A PHILOSOPHER'S SEARCH FOR THE INFINITE

By the same author:

An Augustine Treasury, Boston, 1981.

A PHILOSOPHER'S SEARCH FOR THE INFINITE

Jules M. Brady, S.J.
Professor of Philosophy
Rockhurst College

PHILOSOPHICAL LIBRARY

New York

Imprimi Potest: David L. Fleming, S.J.
Provincial

+ Imprimatur: John J. Sullivan, D.D.
Bishop of Kansas City — St. Joseph

Library of Congress Cataloging in Publication Data

Brady, Jules M.
A philosopher's search for the infinite.

Includes bibliographical references.
1. God—Proof. I. Title.
Bt102.B66 1982 212'.1 81-18889
ISBN 0-8022-2410-5

200 West 57 Street, New York, N.Y. 10019

Manufactured in the United States of America

Dedication:

To Steve, Carol, Stephen,

Mary, Kevin and Glennon Brady

CONTENTS

ACKNOWLEDGMENTS

The author wishes to express his thanks to the following publishers and editor for permission to use their copyright material in this work:

Translation of Psalm 138, published by The Liturgical Press, copyright by The Order of St. Benedict, Inc., Collegeville, Minnesota, used with permission of the publisher.

Translation of St. Thomas' fourth way, by Dr. James F. Anderson, *Treatise on God*, © 1963, p. 11, reprinted by permission of Prentice-Hall, Inc., Englewood Cliffs, New Jersey.

Chapters One, Two, and Four originally appeared in the New Scholasticism: 51 (1977), pp. 1-20; 48 (1974), pp. 219-232; and 38 (1964), pp. 141-158; respectively. Used by permission of the Editor, Dr. Ralph McInerny.

INTRODUCTION

How does a philosopher find God in all things? The answer to this question is given in the four chapters of this book. In the first chapter, philosophical analysis of my own act of knowing the distance between the earth and the moon leads me to conclude that there is a First Efficient Cause of this knowledge. In chapter two, by examining metaphysically the degrees of existing, I come to understand that there is a First Exemplary Cause of these degrees of existing. In chapter three, I propose that my own internal experience of my mind's dynamism affirming a particular existent is the starting point for acknowledging the First Final Cause of that mental appetite. In the fourth chapter, I explain how St. Augustine links all living material things with the First Efficient, Exemplary, and Final Cause. Consequently, whoever understands that each finite being is an effect of the First Cause, whoever mentally runs over limited things, and whoever searches for the Infinite, will surely discover in every being of experience an opening to God. In St. Thomas's view such a person will be performing an act of the habit of wisdom, which disposes an individual to view all finite things as related to the First Cause.[1] Cardinal Newman in *Idea of a University* names this surpassing knowledge an act of the philosophic habit of mind.[2]

In *Perennial Philosophy*, Aldous Huxley suggests that the solution to the problems besetting today's community of nations is neither a particular form of government, nor a gadget produced by technology, nor worldwide fraternal charity but rather the universal admission that each human being depends totally on a Supreme Being.[3] This is the exact opposite of secularism, which maintains that created things do not depend on God.[4] I hope this volume on the philosophical knowledge of God may assist some to come to the realization of their necessary dependence on God.

In *City of God*, St. Augustine quotes Socrates' remark that if the human soul obeys God, the body serves the soul, but if the human spirit forgets its God, the body rebels against the soul from whence originates all the evils in the home and in society.[5] Expressed otherwise, when submission to God is no longer acknowledged by a human person, recognition of the Deity in that person's conscious life is replaced by the pursuit of honor, pleasure, or wealth. In the film *Ordinary People* Conrad says, "I don't believe in God." He unwittingly states the deepest cause for his failure to regulate his lower impulses according to the rule of reason. The connection between control of appetite and knowledge of God is admirably stated in the familiar scripture text "Blessed are the clean of heart for they shall see God."[6]

Footnotes to Introduction

1. S. Thomas Aquinas, *Summa Theol.*, transl. T. Gilby (Garden City, 1959), I, 1, 6 c.
2. J. Newman, *Idea of a University* (Garden City, 1959), p. 160.
3. A. Huxley, *The Perennial Philosophy* (Cleveland, 1962), p. 250.
4. K. Wojtyla, *Sign of Contradiction* (New York, 1979), p. 33.
5. S. Augustine, *City of God*, transl. M. Dods (New York, 1950), p. 246.
6. Matt. 5:8.

CHAPTER ONE

A CONTEMPORARY APPROACH TO GOD'S EXISTENCE

Let us start with a parable. On one occasion a full moon shining through the window of a faculty lounge prompted an astronomer and a metaphysician to discuss the discoveries of the space age. The scientist said, "We now know as a scientific fact that the distance between the moon and the earth is two hundred thirty-nine thousand miles on an average since the orbit of the moon is not a perfect circle." "How do we have such exact knowledge?" the other inquired. The scientist explained the use of the laser beam in computing the precise number of miles. Hearing his colleague's explanation the philosopher admitted, "I too now realize that the moon is two hundred thirty-nine thousand miles from the earth." Then the conversation turned to philosophy with the metaphysician's observation, "The activity itself of knowing the scientific fact about the moon being so many miles from the earth can be the starting point in demonstrating the existence of God."[1] "How can this be done?" the astronomer wondered.

This parable introduces the subject under investigation in this chapter. Note that the question is not whether a scientific fact may be the first step in establishing the existence of God. Rather, the issue is whether knowing the scientific fact can be the initial phase in reasoning to God's existence. In keeping with the parable I shall attempt to answer this question in a way that can be followed by a scientist unfamiliar with philosophical argument.

Demonstrating God's existence from knowing a scientific fact requires the cooperative effort of a scientist and a philosopher. The scientist, by furnishing a scientific fact to be known, provides the first stage of the argument, and the philosopher, by presenting a metaphysical elucidation of this initial step, contributes the remaining stages of the reasoning process. With a scientific fact already given by the astronomer in the above parable, the philosophical analysis will proceed as follows: an analysis of knowing a scientific fact, examination of this analysis, no first cause, first cause, a comparison and conclusion.

An Analysis of Knowing a Scientific Fact

Of the many aspects involved in knowing the distance between the moon and the earth only one will be examined in this study. Anyone knowing this scientific fact will grant that there are at least three aspects of this conscious activity: the objects known, such as the moon and the earth, the human knower, and the act of knowing itself. This analysis will not be pointed toward the objects known, nor toward the subject knowing, but toward the act of scientific knowing. This is to scrutinize the very mystery of human cognitional activity.[2] I will not give an exhaustive account of human knowing, but merely study the act of knowing the scientific fact.

The cognition of the scientific fact about the mileage between the moon and the earth is not an object of sense knowledge. The object of sensory knowledge includes both the six proper sensible objects—color, sound, odor, flavor, temperature, resistance—and the five common sensible objects—extension, motion, rest, shape, and number. All who internally examine their own act of knowing how far the moon is from the earth will admit readily that this cognitive activity is not the pale yellow color of the moon on a clear evening, nor is it sound, odor, flavor, hot or cold, rough or smooth. The same analysis applies to the common sensible objects. All who study their own cognition of the scientific fact given above will surely grant that this cognitive act is not spherical in shape like a full moon, nor is it extended, in motion, at rest, a number. The cognitional act being investigated is simply beyond the object of sensory knowing. In brief, this act of cognition is not an object of sense experience, i.e., an object of external and internal sensation.[3]

Another example of an act of knowing which is not observable by the senses may help here. Although I am aware of my own conscience informing me that to take a magazine from a store rack without paying for it must not be done, this directive given by my conscience is not visible to someone else, nor do I see the conscience internally guiding another person.[4]

Recently, philosophers have emphasized that human knowing activity is not a phenomenon to be investigated by the procedures used in the natural sciences. Rev. Martin C. D'Arcy, S.J. quotes Dr. Ropp's warning that "the scientist who attempts to study the chemistry of thought...resembles a burglar attempting to open a vault of one of the world's largest banks with a toothpick."[5] Eric Mascall, noting that a calculating machine cannot be intelligently self-conscious, rules out "variables in any physical equation which stand for conscious states or activities."[6]

Further analysis reveals that the act of knowing a scientific fact is neither making something nor receiving something.[7] Knowing the earth, the moon, and the distance between them is not the same as producing a work of art from existing material, like Rodin carving the statue of Balzac out of stone. Consequently, a knower in knowing a scientific fact does not change the object known, whereas the artist in creating an art object in some way changes the material used in the process. Cognition about the number of miles between the moon and the earth is different from receiving food. Thus, someone knowing a scientific fact does not destroy the object known, but an animal eating food destroys the object eaten. Therefore, in cognitive activity the known object is neither changed nor destroyed.

Viewed positively, knowing that the moon is two hundred thirty-nine thousand miles from the earth is an existence.[8] First, when I have cognition that the moon is so many miles from the earth, I am aware of the moon, the earth, and the distance between them, i.e., I am present to this scientific fact. Therefore, to know the object in question is to be aware of that object. Secondly, when I come to know that the moon is so far from the earth, I am united with the moon, the earth, and the mileage between them. Hence, knowing the object being studied is in some way a union between the subject and that object. Thirdly, when I have knowledge of the exact expanse between the moon and the earth, in a certain sense, I am the moon, the earth, and the intervening number of miles. It follows that knowing the object is for the knower to be that object. In sum, cognitive activity is to be aware of a scientific fact, a union between the knower and that scientific fact—i.e., simply an existence. If I let a pencil fall from my hand to the top of a desk, I am aware of a falling object; there is a union between me and the moving object; in a sense I am the changing object.

Further analysis discloses that to know a scientific fact is a superexistence. My act of knowing the space mileage between the moon and the earth may be the act of existing by which I exist—the esse that actuates my essence, or it may be the act of existing distinct from the esse by which I am—the esse which actuates my nature. The first alternative is unsatisfactory because to grant it is to admit no distinction between merely existing as a human person and existing as knowing a scientific fact. To accept the second alternative is to assign to my cognition of this scientific fact a better act of existing,[9] an intentional esse, a cognitional existence, a superexistence.

Thus far I have established the following: A cognitive act is not an object of external or internal sensation; it neither changes nor destroys the object known; such knowing is to be aware of an object, a union between knower and known, an act of existing, even a superexistence.[10]

Examination of this Analysis

What type of cognition is employed when I proceed from being aware of how far the moon is from the earth to knowing the intentional esse of my cognition about this distance? In other words, from an initial stage of knowing a certain scientific fact there is a transition to knowing the cognitional esse of that knowing; we inquire neither about cognition in the initial stage nor about cognition in the final stage, but about naming the method of cognition conducting us throughout all three aspects of this cognitional transition: the start, the change, and the result.

Our search will consist in considering which one of the following three knowledge methods is most adequate. These ways of knowing are direct knowledge, reflexive knowledge, and introspective knowledge.

Direct knowledge disqualifies because it is too narrow in scope to cover the transition from cognition of the scientific fact to knowing the esse of that cognition.

Witnessing that the sun warms the stone,[11] an instance of direct knowing, is knowledge of an object that is beyond what is knowable by the external senses and includes what can be known by these senses. The connection between the sun and the stone is neither a proper nor common sensible object, and, hence, is not known by the external senses, whereas the color of the sun and the warmth of the stone can be known by the senses. Therefore, direct knowledge, according to the point of view taken in this study, is cognition of an object some of whose components are knowable by the external senses.[12]

When we apply this type of knowledge to the cognitional transition being discussed, direct cognition clearly applies to the initial stage namely, knowing that two hundred thirty-nine thousand miles intervene between moon and earth. Although the exact distance between the moon and the earth cannot be known by the external senses alone, the color and shape of the moon are known by these same senses. But direct knowledge does not fit the last stage of this cognitive transition: knowing the existence of cognition about this scientific fact, because this latter knowledge itself is not an object some of whose components are sensible, and hence the esse of this knowing activity is not such an object.

Reflexive knowledge also is not an apt vehicle for describing the cognitive transition from cognition of a scientific fact to cognition of the existence of that knowledge. However, it is not as easy to rule out reflexive knowledge as it is to rule out direct knowledge. For one thing different philosophers define reflexive knowledge differently. The difficulty diminishes, however, if we restrict reflexive knowledge to mean inadvertent knowing of direct cognition, adding that we perform the former in the very act by which we perform the latter. To put it another way, direct cognition is a double awareness: awareness of an object some of whose components can be known by the external senses, and inadvertent awareness of the direct cognition itself.[13] This latter awareness is what we mean by reflexive knowledge.

Suppose we ask a spectator in a theatre during a performance of Shakespeare's King Lear two questions. "Are you aware that you are knowing the plot of the drama as it unfolds? Before you were asked, were you deliberately adverting to the fact that you are aware of this knowledge?'' No doubt, the first question would receive an affirmative reply, and the second question would be answered negatively. In the latter case, the spectator's inadvertent awareness of his own knowledge of the stage play being enacted is an instance of reflexive knowledge.

A comparison of reflexive cognition and the cognitive change being considered reveals that reflexive knowledge corresponds with the initial stage of the intentional change but not with the final stage. Reflexive cognition is certainly another facet of the starting point, i.e., direct knowledge of the distance intervening between the moon and the earth, since by reflexive knowledge we are inadvertently aware of this direct cognition in the very act by which we know the scientific fact. However, reflexive knowledge does not extend to the result of the cognitive transition that concerns us: knowing the esse of directly knowing a scientific fact. The object of reflexive cognition is only the direct cognition of a certain scientific fact and not the intentional esse of the direct knowledge. Of course, if we ask our imaginary theatre patron a final question, ''Are you aware that you are knowing the superexistence of knowing the dramatic plot?'' the answer surely will be negative.

Introspective knowledge, finally, is a suitable instrument for embracing all three stages of the cognitive transition that interests us. As with reflexive knowledge, thinkers do not define the act of introspecting exactly the same way.[14] Once again, as with reflexive knowledge, we shall confine introspective knowledge to signify a deliberate turning from direct cognition to knowing a characteristic of that cognition.[15]

The three stages of introspective knowledge—the direct cognition, the deliberate turning,[16] and knowing an aspect of direct knowing—can be easily verified in the following example. Upon being questioned a student will readily admit that the desk in front of the room is heavier and longer than a pencil in the instructor's hand. This, of course, provides an instance of direct cognition. After further inquiry the student will also grant that his act of knowing about the desk being heavier and longer than the pencil is itself without weight and without size. Thus, the student knows a characteristic of his own direct cognition. Obviously, it was at the urging of the teacher that the student freely turned from a direct cognition of a quantitative comparison to knowing a characteristic of that direct knowledge. Measuring this tripartite definition of introspection by the three moments of the cognitional motion that concerns us manifests that the former admirably conforms to the latter. The passage itself from knowing the scientific fact to knowing the existence of that knowing is certainly a deliberate transition. And surely knowing the exact intervening distance between the moon and the earth is direct cognition. Lastly, knowing the superexistence of that space knowledge is an aspect of the original direct cognition. In retrospect, passing from direct cognition of a scientific fact to an awareness of the intentional *esse* of that cognition is not direct knowledge, nor reflexive knowledge, but introspective knowledge.

The work of classifying the cognitive processes serving thus far in our demonstration of God's existence would be incomplete if at this point we did not indicate that both direct cognition of exactly how far the moon is from the earth as well as knowing the existence of that cognition are acts of thinking or of intellection. By now it is easy to establish that directly knowing the scientific fact mentioned is an act of thinking by pointing out that this direct cognition is at the same time reflexive knowledge, which cannot be said of an act of sensation like seeing the white color of this page.[17] No one would admit seeing an act of seeing the white color of this paper. And so, seeing is not simultaneously reflexive cognition. On the other hand, knowing the esse of the direct awareness of the same scientific fact is an act of intellection, since sensation always attains a proper sensible object and the intentional existence of direct cognition is beyond all the proper sensible objects. In other words, reflexive knowledge and knowing esse, two kinds of cognition not found in sensation, are verified in a direct cognitional act and in knowing the existence of that cognition respectively. Thus an act of direct cognition and knowing the *esse* of direct knowledge are better acts of knowing than sensation. We name these better cognitive acts thinking or intellection.[18] To sum up, our demonstration, then, begins with two acts of intellection, direct thinking about a certain scientific fact evolving into introspective thinking about the existence of that direct thinking.

No First Cause

The central question in our enterprise of demonstrating God's existence concerns not the first stage in the procedure, directly thinking about the two hundred thirty-nine thousand miles between the moon and the earth, but the second stage, introspecting the *esse* of the previous direct intellection. Does the existence of thinking about this scientific fact depend ultimately on Absolute Existence?[19] Can the intentional *esse* of intellectually knowing the length of a journey between the earth and the moon be fully explained only by Pure *Esse*? Is the *superesse* of direct intellection about this scientific fact ultimately grounded only in Absolute *Esse*?

Whoever considers why four philosophers would respond negatively to the central question just formulated will be better prepared to understand why a realist answers this key question affirmatively.[20] This would be especially true of someone unacquainted with philosophical thinking, like the astronomer in the parable at the beginning of this study. For this reason we now explain briefly why Plato, Kant, a Positivist and Nagel would not admit that we can know the ultimate dependence of intentional *esse* on the actual influence of Pure *Esse*. (No one is denying, of course, that these thinkers have contributed substantially to man's understanding of himself and his environment. But with regard to accounting for cognitional existence they are mute.)

Plato's philosophy can't deal with the question about the ultimate ground of intentional *esse* because Platonism is a philosophy of essences. In his famous dialogues Plato, in order to establish that true reality is a world of Separated Ideas, Forms, or Essences, applied a presupposition from Parmenides to definitions. What is thought is what is, Parmenides had said. Since what is thought is a concept and what is is reality, Plato concluded that concept, or definition, corresponds perfectly with reality. Noticing that any definition, like that of a triangle, is immaterial, immutable, infinite, necessary and universal, Plato used the correspondence principle to argue that true reality, such as the reality of a triangle, is likewise immaterial, immutable, infinite, necessary and universal. This reality is a Separated Idea, Form or Essence. In the *Republic*, Plato wrote that we assume an Idea whenever we apply the same name to many separate things.[21] However, this entire procedure applies only to essence, since a definition is the mental expression of an essence and the Separated Idea is also an Essence. Intentional existence is not an essence and therefore is excluded from the Platonic analysis.

Among other reasons, Kant's notion of being makes it impossible for his philosophy to account for the ultimate cause of intentional being. What is his notion of being? Being, he said, is not a real predicate,[22] a synthetic predicate, one that not only adds to the subject, but also enlarges it.[23] For instance, "warms" is such a predicate in the proposition "The sun warms the stone."[24] Rather, being is either a category or experience. As a category, being is a copula, a logical predicate, one that adds nothing to the subject but merely posits the subject and all its predicates as in the proposition "A triangle is a three-angled figure."[25] "Is" in the proposition just given signifies 'is' as a category. Being as experience, however, does not enlarge the subject, but does add an additional possible perception.[26] Now a perception for Kant is an appearance combined with consciousness.[27] And appearance is a synthesis of sensation in general and the sense forms of space and time.[28] In the following example given by Kant, 'real' refers to something that exists as experience. "My financial condition is affected differently by a hundred real dollars than it is by a hundred possible dollars."[29]

From this explanation it follows that neither 'is' as a category nor 'is' as experience has the same meaning as intentional existence. The function of 'is' as a category is to connect the subject and the predicate in an analytic proposition, while intentional esse describes the thinking activity itself. 'Is' as experience, however, includes among other components, sensation in general, sense form of space and the sense form of time. But the intentional act of existing, as was said before, is in no way sensible. Therefore intentional esse is outside the notion of being presented in the *Critique of Pure Reason*. And this Kantian notion, accordingly, cannot help in discovering the ultimate source of intentional esse.

Because of his view that the human mind is open only to one level of truth, the realm of knowledge based on scientific facts, a Positivist is of no assistance in the search for the ultimate ground of intentional being. Why would a Positivist deny plural levels of truth? One explanation is that he has pursued research into scientific facts, i.e., facts established immediately or mediately by scientific observation,[30] so exclusively that he is closed to any other level of truth.[31] Be that as it may, a Positivist would maintain consistently that questions about another level of truth, philosophical facts, i.e., facts arising from a philosophical analysis of experience, like the existence of motion, the existence of things, the existence of thought,[32] are meaningless. And so, intentional esse, not a scientific fact but a philosophical fact, has no meaning for a Positivist. Here we certainly do not condemn a scientist who refuses to exchange the scientist's cap for the philosopher's cap and ask a philosophical question. But we do have misgivings about any thinker who will not allow the human mind to search for the answer to a philosophical question.[33]

With empirical evidence supporting his double-level theory of reality, Ernest Nagel constructs a philosophy of naturalism[34] in which the question about whether Absolute Existence ultimately grounds intentional existence is without meaning. He opts for the empirical method since it seems to be the most reliable way of knowing there is.[35] Moreover, naturalism maintains that reality is twofold, including not only material bodies and organizations of material bodies but also what is beyond these bodies and their organizations, namely, *forms* of behavior and *functions* of material systems such as modes of action, plans, aspirations. But, although forms and functions are parts of nature, they are not agents that bring themselves or others into concrete reality.[36] Thus naturalism has no room for an immaterial mind guiding the course of events.[37] Since cognitional existence cannot be classified as a material system, naturalism has no room for it either.

First Cause

A scientist, uninitiated in the ways of philosophy, wondering about whether intentional esse depends on the actual influence of Absolute *Esse*, noticing the reasons why Platonism, Kantianism, positivism and naturalism cannot deal with the question, might be inclined to consider why a realist claims to answer this pivotal question. To serve this purpose a realist might propose the following argument by exclusion. Either intentional existence has no sufficient reason, or it is completely explained by the essence of the human being exercising this intentional act of existing, or it is fully accounted for by the substantial *esse* of the human person performing this intellectual activity, or it is ultimately grounded by the sum total of all the degrees of existing, the degrees of existing possessed by all finite beings, or it is fully intelligible by Pure *Esse*. Since being is intelligible, and since the above disjunction is complete, if the first four members of the disjunction are found to be unintelligible, Unlimited *Esse* will be the correct answer to the question.

Of course, the first solution, the attempt to ground the intentional act of existing in no sufficient reason, is unacceptable because, for a realist, being is intelligible. Considering this initial solution to the question and its unsuitability reminds us that the principle of sufficient reason or intelligibility, not the principle of contradiction, is at the root of this demonstration of God's existence.[38]

The second answer, the essence of the human person who has the cognitional esse we are investigating, cannot account for this cognitional existence. Evidently a human being is not identical with another existing rational animal. From this it follows that a human person does not contain the whole perfection of existing but rather is deficient or limited in the perfection of being. Now the function of essence, an intrinsic principle of being, is precisely to explain this deficiency, this limitation in the perfection of being. In a phrase, essence in a human person is potency in the order of existing. And surely the effort to ground human intellection, a new perfection of existing, by the human essence, a potential principle, is clearly contradictory. It is germane here to note the realist's contention that we intellectually apprehend the essence of a human person while we intellectually affirm our own cognitional esse.

Thirdly, the substantial *esse* of a human person does not adequately explain the intentional esse exercised by that same person. Of course the substantial act of existing and the intentional act of existing of a human subject are both similar and different. They are similar inasmuch as both are not complete beings but rather components of a human being, intrinsic principles of being, perfections in the reason of being. But they account for different perfections in a rational being.

Substantial esse is the intrinsic component by which a human subject exists, while intentional esse is the intrinsic principle by which a human being is intentionally an object.

Now, measuring a person who merely exists by the same person existing with an intentional act of existing discredits the substantial esse as the total explanation of an intentional esse in the same individual. For an existing person who is intentionally an object exists in a better way than the same person merely existing. That is to say, a human being possessing substantial esse and cognitional esse exists in a better manner than the same being merely having substantial esse. So, a person existing as a thinking adult exists in a better degree than he did when he was a newly born infant. But to say that the substantial esse of a human person is the total reason of the intentional esse in that same being is to claim that an inferior degree of existing totally explains a superior degree of existing. This is unintelligible. An analogy may help here. A bean plant growing green leaves exists in a better way than the same plant living with white leaves. No botanist would claim that the plant itself is the total cause of the green color of the plant's leaves, since a plant grown entirely in a dark room develops white leaves. If it is placed in the sunlight the leaves begin turning green.

In the fourth place, the sum total of degrees of existing is not the ultimate ground for the intentional act of existing exercised by a human person whose substantial esse is within the sum total of those degrees. The argument by comparing degrees of existing also applies here. The sum total of grades of existing and the intentional esse proceeding from a human person existing within the grades exist in a better way than the same sum total of degrees without that intentional esse. To insist that the sum total of the degrees of existing without intentional esse is the ultimate ground for the sum total of degrees of being with the intentional act of being is to take the view that an inferior degree of existing totally grounds a superior grade of being. Once again, this is not intelligible.

With the first four members of the complete disjunction discarded, and since we admit that there is a sufficient reason for intentional esse, it follows that Pure *Esse* is this sufficient reason. In other words, intentional existence does depend on the actual influence of Pure Existence, the perfection of being beyond the grades in its infinite perfection, the act of existing containing in itself the whole perfection of existing, the First Efficient Cause.

Since the above disjunctive syllogism has provided the last two stages in our proposed demonstration of God's existence, all four stages of the complete argument can now be assembled. First stage: we know that the moon is two hundred thirty-nine thousand miles from the earth, a scientific fact. Second stage: the act of thinking this distance between the moon and the earth is an intentional esse, which is a philosophical fact known by introspective analysis. Third stage: but this intentional act of existing ultimately depends on the actual influence of Pure *Esse*, the First Efficient Cause. Fourth stage: therefore this First Cause, Pure *Esse*, is. As we have seen, the third stage, a causal proposition, has been established by a disjunctive syllogism.

A Comparison

When we compare intentional esse and Pure *Esse*, additional features of the demonstration just completed appear. Intentional existence is a component, an intrinsic principle of a limited person; Pure Existence is being. In a human being substantial esse and cognitional esse cannot be divided into two beings but nevertheless are really distinct; in God substantial esse and intellection are identical because intellection is a superexistence while Pure *Esse*, as we have established, is Infinite, containing in itself the whole perfection of existing.[39] As we indicated above, intentional esse is not an object of sensory experience; nor is Absolute *Esse* an object of sense experience.[40] Rather, by using philosophical analysis we introspect the existence of our own direct intellection. On the other hand, at the conclusion of our proof we know that Pure *Esse* is, inasmuch as we affirm that the proposition "Absolute *Esse* is" is true. The evidence for this proposition is simply that Pure Existence is the ultimate ground for cognitional esse.[41] Finally, an intentional act of existing is an effect since it is a new perfection of existing in comparison with substantial esse; Pure *Esse* is the First Efficient Cause actually influencing through the human person, who is the secondary efficient cause, the cognitional existence of that person. Undoubtedly the human knower is an efficient cause of his own cognition. After all, he is the one who is performing the act of knowing.[42]

How God and man influence intentional *esse* is as mysterious as how God and man produce a human free act.[43] But Josef Pieper reminds us not to be dismayed at this. Science, he says, in principle can answer fully the questions it asks, while philosophy can never finally answer its questions.[44] The poet writes about this mysterious union of God and human knowledge.

> "O Lord, you have probed me and you know me;
> you know when I sit and when I stand;
> You understand my thoughts from afar.
> My journeys and my rest you scrutinize,
> with all my ways you are familiar.
> Even before a word is on my tongue,
> behold, O Lord, you know the whole of it.
> Behind me and before me, you hem me in
> and rest your hand upon me.
> Such knowledge is too wonderful for me;
> too lofty for me to attain."[45]

Conclusion

Is this chapter appropriately entitled "A Contemporary

Approach to God's Existence?" It seems so for two reasons. In the first step of the proof, the use of the laser beam established the scientific fact about the exact distance between the moon and the earth. This fact, in turn, specified the direct act of thinking which is the launching pad for this way to God. The second stage of the demonstration developed in this essay used the "turn to the transcendental method",[46] which was made famous by Kant in his *Critique of Pure Reason*, influencing the whole of post-Kantian philosophy, and has been practiced by the Transcendental Thomists. This method consists in turning our attention from the object to our cognition of it. In the second step of our argument for God's existence we turned from direct intellection of a scientific fact to know the *esse* of that intellection.[47] Because of these two procedures, direct cognition of a scientific fact and introspecting the *esse* of that cognition, we think that the title of this essay is justified. Has not this inquiry established that our own direct human thinking is a sign of the existence of God?

Footnotes to Chapter One:

1. For an approach to God's existence with a similar starting point cf. Jean-Dominique Robert, O.P., *Approche Contemporaine d'une Affirmation de Dieu* (Bruges, 1962), pp. 9-221.

2. Two authors assert that Kant considered only the content of knowing, not the activity itself of human knowing. E. Coreth, S.J., *Metaphysics*, transl. J. Donceel, S.J. (New York, 1968), p. 52. J. Donceel, S.J., "A Case in Reason for God's Existence," in *God Knowable and Unknowable*, ed. R.J. Roth, S.J. (New York, 1973), p. 174.

3. Notice the following description of experience in J. Marechal, S.J., "Au Seuil de la Metaphysique: Abstraction ou Intuition," in *Melanges Joseph Marechal*, Tome I, *Oeuvres* (Paris, 1950), p. 117. "We place ourselves now outside of metaphysics, at the heart of that immediate and concrete knowledge which our external and internal senses acquire and which we generally call experience." Transl. J.M.B.

4. This example is taken from St. Augustine, *On the Gospel of John*, in *A Select Library of the Nicene and Post-Nicene Fathers*, vol. 7, ed. P. Schaff (New York, 1887-1892), p. 335.

5. *Dialogue with Myself* (New York, 1966), p. 86.

6. *The Openness of Being* (Philadelphia, 1971), p. 262.

7. This negative analysis is from J. Maritain, *The Degrees of Knowledge*, transl. G. B. Phelan (New York, 1959), pp. 111-115.

8. This positive analysis is adpated from J. Maritain, *ibid*.

9. "Better" more appropriately describes the perfection of existing here than "bigger." Cf. below, Chap. Two.

10. A study of pertinent texts in Aquinas reveals that for the Angelic Doctor cognition is the existence of the thing known in the knower, according to an article by J. Owens, C.S.S.R., "Cognition as Existence," in the *Proceedings of the American Catholic Philosophical Association,* XLVIII (1974), 75.

11. This example is given by I. Kant, *Prolegomena to Any Future Metapysics*, ed. L. Beck (Indianapolis, 1950), p. 49.

12. Compare this definition with the following definition of perception given by E. Mascall, *op. cit*., p. 99. Perception is the direct, mediated activity in which the intellect in and through the sensible particular grasps the intelligible, extra-mental being. Likewise compare our definition of direct knowledge with the following description of direct cognition stated by V.J. Bourke in his article "Invalid Proofs for God's Existence," in the *Proceedings of the American Catholic Philosophical Association,* XXVIII (1954), 37. Using both sense powers and intellect we first directly grasp bodily things existing extra-mentally.

13. Cf. Mascall, *op. cit*., p. 46.

14. In his *Method in Theology* (New York, 1972), p. 8, B. Lonergan, S.J. cautions that introspection is not an inward ocular glance.

15. Cf. Mascall, *op. cit*., p. 46.

16. Coreth calls this the turn to the transcendental method in which we turn our attention from the object to our cognition of it. *Op. cit*., p. 23.

17. CF. J. Marechal, S.J., A *Marechal Reader*, transl. and ed. J. Donceel, S.J. (New York, 1970), p. 203. Sensibility, an intrinsically material knowing power, is not a self-transparent faculty.

18. For other types of intellectual activity cf. Lonergan, *op. cit*., p. 15.

19. Robert, *op. cit*., pp. 204-205, proposes the question of his study as follows. How does one ultimately harmonize these paradoxical aspects revealed in scientific truth: a contingently existing act of human thought considering necessary intelligibilities creates one scientific truth which is in many minds?

20. Man has an unquenchable thirst for knowledge according to J. De Finance, S.J., *Essai sur L'Agir Humain* (Rome, 1962), p. 125.

21. *Rep*., X, 596a.

22. I. Kant, *Critique of Pure Reason*, transl. N. Smith (New York, 1933), p. 504.

23. *Ibid.*

24. *Prolegomena to Any Future Metaphysics, op. cit.*, p. 49.

25. *Critique of Pure Reason, op. cit.*, pp. 504, 502.

26. *Ibid.*, p. 506.

27. *Ibid.*, p. 143.

28. *Ibid.*, p. 82.

29. *Ibid.*, p. 505.

30. Cf. Maritain, *op. cit.*, p. 58.

31. Cf. Robert, *op. cit.*, p. 155

32. Cf. Maritain, *op. cit.*, p. 57.

33. Cf. Robert, *op. cit.*, pp. 139-140.

34. "Naturalism Reconsidered," in *Contemporary Philosophic Problems*, ed. Y. Krikorian and A. Edel (New York, 1959), pp. 337-349.

35. *Ibid.*, p. 344.

36. *Ibid.*, p. 340.

37. *Ibid.*

38. This view is proposed by N. Clark, S.J., "Analytic Philosophy and Language about God," in *Christian Philosophy and Religious Renewal*, ed. G. McLean, O.M.I. (Washington, 1967), pp. 48 f.

39. Cf. Maritain, *op. cit.*, p. 113.

40. Experiencing is the same as being conscious according to Lonergan, *op. cit.*, pp. 6-20. In this view sensory experiencing and mental experiencing would be the same as being sensorially conscious and being mentally conscious respectively.

41. Cf. Coreth, *op. cit.*, p. 29. Infinite Being is never revealed to us as an object, but it is known by us only in the finite beings whose ground it is.

42. Cf. Owens, *op. cit.*, p. 81.

43. Cf. Robert, *op. cit.*, p. 186.

44. *Leisure the Basis of Culture*, transl. A. Dru (New York, 1963), p. 106.

45. *Psalm* 138, transl. The Liturgical Press (Collegeville, 1961).

46. Coreth, *op. cit.*, p. 23.

47. Transcendental method functions similarly in the *Critique of Pure Reason* and in our essay because both demand a turning from the object. But there is a difference. Kant turns to examine the way we know objects. *Op. cit.*, p. 59. In this study we turn to affirm the intentional esse of direct intellection.

CHAPTER TWO

NOTE ON THE FOURTH WAY

This chapter attempts to clarify the reasoning process in Thomas Aquinas's fourth way by using a triple procedure: raising a question about different degrees of existing, comparing a grade of existing with quantity and examining an objection. Certainly any effort toward making the fourth proof of the existence of God more intelligible, or less unintelligible, seems worthy of merit.

Accordingly, the initial aim of this meditation will be to account for the similarity between a human act of existing and a brute act of existing, different degrees of being. They are similar because both the human *esse* and the brute *esse* are perfections of existing. Yet they differ since a human entitative act is superior to an animal's ontological act. For whoever admits that as a being exists so does it act, and whoever accepts that human intellection is a strictly immaterial activity while sensation, the highest operation of a brute, is in some way material, will grant the truth of the proposition not that man is a better man than an animal, not that man is a better animal than a brute, but simply that he has an ontological act which is better than the ontological perfection of an irrational animal.[1] The question raised in this discussion, then, is how do we ultimately explain that a human existential act and a brute existential act, dissimilar degrees of existing, are alike. Surely, this is a tantalizing puzzle.

Due to its abstruse character the point at issue here must be made more precise. In Aristotle's philosophy of nature two men are similar as men for the reason that each essence has an intrinsic actual principle, substantial form.[2] And it is consistent with Aquinas's philosophy of being to maintain that a man and a brute are similar as being inasmuch as there is a transcendental relation between essence and existence in each of these beings. The question of this study, then, is not how to ground the similarity between two human beings as men, not what is the basis for the resemblance between a man and a brute as being, but what the credentials are for acknowledging the likeness between the act of existing of a man and the act of existing of a brute—which are different degrees of being. Expressed in different language, this analysis takes up the problem of the one and the many in regard to grades of existence. How can a human existential perfection and a brute existential act be both one insofar as they resemble each other and many insofar as they are diverse? Indeed this is a profound metaphysical consideration.

Further light on the topic under scrutiny can be gained by comparing a real relation of quantity with a real relation of similarity in existing. To affirm that a yardstick is bigger than a one-foot ruler is to ascribe to them a real relation of quantity. Now any real relation of comparison minimally requires three things: a real subject, that which is ordered to the term; a real term, that to which the subject is ordered; and a real foundation, that which accounts for the similarity between the subject and the term. Obviously, in this quantitative proportion the subject, the term and the foundation are the yardstick, the ruler and their dimensions respectively.[3] But to say that a man exists in a better way than a brute does, is to attribute to them a real relation of similarity in existing. Although it is easy to see that in this relation the subject and the term are the man and the brute, it is not so easy to see what the foundation might be. For the foundation in this evaluation must account for the similarity between a human entitative act and a brute perfection of existing. And this is exactly the question at hand. Hence the first topic of this study may be phrased in another way. What is the foundation for the real relation of similarity-in-existing between a man and a brute?

The method of research that will yield a satisfactory answer to these ontological questions can only be a reflection on our own knowledge of being. Since being is intelligible, if all the possible solutions—1) essence of a limited being, 2) human esse, 3) human esse and brute esse taken together, 4) the sum total of degrees of existing—furnished by limited beings are discovered to be unsatisfactory because they involve a contradiction, it follows that Unlimited Being will remain as the adequate explanation. This reflection, at this point, will consider the following topics: Inadequate Solutions, the Adequate Solution and a Demonstration.

Inadequate Solutions

The first solution suggested, the essence of a finite being, either of man or of brute, disqualifies as the ground for the parity between the variegated grades of existing in man and in an animal because such an essence is a passive potency in the order of existing, a capacity for receiving an act of existing. And to affirm that the ability to receive an act of existing is a sufficient reason for the resemblance between these existential perfections is to say that passive potency, the limiting principle, explains act, the perfecting principle. This would be a contradiction.

The human esse, the second solution proposed, also fails

to meet the criterion of intelligibility. Of course, the human entitative act insofar as it ontologically excels the brute act of existing explains why the former differs from the latter. But to employ the human perfection of existing also to account for their likeness is to claim that the human *esse* and the brute *esse* differ and are similar under the same respect, again a contradiction. In like manner no Aristotelian would write that two men differ and are alike due to prime matter, an intrinsic potential principle in every human essence. It would be unthinkable for the judge in a music festival, after declaring one tenor's rendition of the Toreador song more perfect than that of another contestant's, to decide that the two vocalists tied for first place since their achievements were so similar.

In the third place, neither will the human existential perfection and the brute existential act taken together do as the ultimate basis for their mutual similarity. Again, because man's act of existing is a higher ontological value than a brute's perfection of existing, evidently both existential degrees taken together ground their reciprocal difference. However, to base this difference and this similarity on these entitative acts taken together is to state that they differ and are similar according to the same respect, another contradiction. Yet it is otherwise when measuring a yardstick and a one-foot ruler against each other. They are alike and different according to their dimensions without implying a contradiction. While they correspond perfectly for twelve inches, the additional twenty-four inches in the longer measure differ completely from the absence of any quantity beyond one foot in the smaller ruler.

Fourthly, the sum total of degrees of existing is of no help in resolving the problem. As it is itself a degree of existing, the sum total of grades of existing is subject to the same difficulty that besets the human entitative act as the explanatory principle of the resemblance under investigation. Whereas the existential act of man and the existential act of an animal differ mutually due to these acts themselves, the reason for their mutual similarity is not the sum total of the degrees of existence, because the degrees intervening between an animal act of existing and the sum total of the degrees differ from the grades ranging between a human act of existing and the sum total of the grades. An example brings out the point here. After three art students have each painted a copy of the original Mona Lisa, suppose the instructor assigns grades of seventy, eighty, ninety to the student paintings. Surely the pictures that receive the two lowest grades differ from each other. Yet no one would claim that the reason for their mutual similarity is the remaining student painting, since obviously the numerical value between seventy and ninety is greater than between seventy and eighty.

Adequate Solution

With all the possible explanations from finite beings investigated and found unsatisfactory, and granting that being is intelligible, the question is finally answered by Unlimited Being. The affirmation that there is an act of existing without limit, the act of existing beyond the degrees in its infinite perfection, the perfection of existing containing in itself the whole perfection of existing is the ultimate reason for the likeness between man's existence and a brute's existence. While these degrees differ and are many due to their differing grades of existing, they are similar and are one on account of Pure *Esse*, which is imitated by each degree albeit differently. In other words, the infinite entitative act, the exemplar, resembled in different ways by the differing grades of existing, the exemplates, is the correct foundation for the real relation of similarity between man's perfection of existing and a brute's existential act. Thus the different degrees of existing resemble each other because they all resemble the illimited act of existing.

An example from art parallels this solution. Just as two paintings of the Mona Lisa awarded different grades by an art teacher are similar insofar as they both imitate the original picture, which is beyond grading, so a man's act of existing and an animal's act of existing are alike because they imitate Infinite *Esse*, which is beyond the degrees. Of course, this is only an analogy. It is with the eye of the body that one sees the copies and the original painting. But it is only with the eye of the mind that one affirms the act of existing in a limited being, i.e., the effect and the truth of the proposition that there is pure act of existing, the First Exemplary Cause.

A Demonstration

The entire preceding analysis can be epitomized in a syllogism demonstrating the existence of God from the different degrees of existing. First step: a human act of existing is superior to a brute act of existing. Second step: but superiority is affirmed of a human *esse* in comparison with a brute *esse* since they both imitate differently the infinite act of existing. Conclusion: Therefore there is an infinite act of existing. The evidence for the premises of this argument has already been presented in the first part of this chapter. As confirmation of this evidence, consider that the human *esse* and the brute *esse* are degrees, not of human existence, not of human and brute existence taken together, not of the sum total of the existential grades, but of the act of existing itself.

Since the structured proof above is a particularization of Aquinas's argument of the fourth way, Thomas's text is given here.

> "The *fourth way* is taken from the grades (of perfection) found in things. Among beings there are some more and some less good, true, and noble; and so in the case of other perfections of this kind. But 'more' and 'less' are predicated of diverse things according as they approach

in diverse measures something which is the maximum, as a thing is found hotter the more it approaches that which is hottest. There is, then, something which is truest and best and noblest and, consequently, something which is maximally a being. For those things that are greatest in truth are greatest in being, as Aristotle says in Book II of the *Metaphysics*."[4]

Part and Grade

Just as a comparison of a real relation of quantity with a real relation of similarity between different degrees of existential acts assisted in the elaboration of the previous inquiry, so a contrast of a part of quantity with a degree of the entitative act will be the second means of elucidating the fourth way dialectic. Hence the differences between part and grade, described by the late Rev. Aloisius Korinek, S.J.[5] in his recently privately printed book on natural theology, will disclose the meaning of a perfection which is used in the fourth way, i.e., one whose notion contains no imperfection. His ensemble of the six ways in which a part and a grade differ will now be explained. First of all, the quantitative aspect of beings but not their entitative aspect can be added together. A yardstick can be assembled by joining a twelve-inch ruler with a twenty-four inch measure. But a brute act of existing does not result from splicing together a plant act of existing with another act of existing.[6] Secondly, adjectives appropriately modifying the perfection of quantity are not the same as those adequately describing the perfection of being. A yardstick is not qualitatively better than but quantitatively bigger than a one-foot ruler; whereas brute existence is not quantitatively bigger than but qualitatively better than plant existence.[7]

Thirdly, divisibility applies to a body possessing quantity, a lateral perfection found in all material things, but not to the act of existing, a vertical perfection present in all beings.

Thus a yardstick is a quantified body with potential parts. But the entitative act of a brute is a simple quality without parts.[8] Fourthly, the word "part" applies to a quantified object while the word "degree" or "grade" fits the qualitative perfection of being. For example, a yardstick is a part of quantity. On the other hand, a brute act of being is a degree or grade of esse.[9]

Fifthly, our way of knowing the foundation of a real relation of quantity differs from our way of knowing the foundation of a real relation of similarity in existing. The act of comparing two quantified objects includes explicit knowledge of quantity before further analysis leads to the explicit affirmation of quantity as the foundation for the comparison. This prior explicit knowledge is both sensation of extension or quantity as a common sensible object and intellectual apprehension objectively representing these dimensions or quantity. On the other hand, affirming the similarity between different grades of entitative act contains no explicit but only implicit knowledge of maximal being, before further examination yields a demonstration which concludes with the explicit affirmation of the infinite ontological act as the foundation for the likeness. There is no prior explicit knowledge of Pure *Esse* because neither sensing, nor intellectual apprehending, nor existential affirming attains the pure act of existing. There is no sensation of Infinite *Esse* because both the proper sensible objects, what can be known by only one sense power, and the common sensible objects, what can be known by more than one sense power but only through a proper sensible object, do not embrace existence. Neither is there apprehension of the unlimited act of existing since material essence, the object of the first act of the mind, is not the act of existing. Nor, finally, is there existential affirmation of the infinite act of existing. The reason is that the act of existing of a material being, the object of the existential judgment, is not Pure *Esse*. An example summarizes this absence of explicit knowledge of the highest being. A student once said, "I don't hear existence." To be more complete he should have said, "I don't sense, nor apprehend, but I do existentially affirm the act of existing of a limited, material being.[10] But I neither sense, nor apprehend, nor existentially judge Pure *Esse*." However, according to Korinek, the act of affirming that different degrees of existing are alike does involve implicit knowledge of Pure *Esse*.

What is this implicit knowledge? Maximal being is prefigured or implicitly affirmed in every act of comparing the existential grades of being.[11] That is to say, the intellect affirming the existence of a limited being tends or is dynamically oriented towards the infinite because the affirmation of such an act of existing does not satisfy the intellect. What is the explanation of this dissatisfaction? The formal object of the intellect is being as being. And judging the existence of sensible being does not completely exhaust the formal object of the intellect since the intellect can affirm limitation of such a being. Consequently, it is because affirming existence of a limited being does not wholly expend the formal object of the intellect that such an affirmation fails to satisfy the tendency of the intellect. On the other hand, the affirmation of the truth of the plenitude of being completely fills up the formal object of the intellect since the intellect cannot affirm limitation of the truth of this being. And so, it is for the reason that judging the truth of the plentitude of being fully realizes the formal object of the intellect that this judgment satisfies the tendency of the intellect.[12] Scientific research is an example of the implicit knowledge under study. Dr. Salk, searching for a medicine to prevent polio, implicitly knew polio vaccine. This vaccine as the term of a tendency was virtually present in the tendency of the scientist seeking a compound to eliminate polio. Of course, this is only an analogy. For one thing, the outcome of the demonstration of God's existence is a proposition known to be true because of evidence given in the fourth way.[13] Whereas the experiments of the scientist resulted in the discovery of a vaccine which can be verified by controlled sensory observation.

Sixthly and finally, a direct mutual comparison of two bodies differing in size warrants judging that one is longer than the other; but an indirect comparison of different entitative degrees with the infinite act of existing is the basis for recognizing, during the first step of the fourth proof, the similarity between these different grades of existing. On the one hand, direct measuring of a yardstick and a one-foot ruler by each other is possible because the intellect, throughout the entire process of measuring, explicitly knows the univocal quantity which is common to both items used. On the other hand, while direct reciprocal measuring of human *esse* and brute *esse* is impossible since the act of existing is an analogous perfection intrinsic to man and brute, the indirect comparing of these different existential degrees with maximal being in the initial phase of the fourth way is possible because the intellect in the early stage of the argument has implicit knowledge of maximal being and only at the conclusion of the reasoning process in the proof achieves explicit knowledge of the supreme being. Therefore this indirect comparing is measuring the grades of being with the infinite act of existing not explicitly affirmed as true at the conclusion of the demonstration but implicitly affirmed in every affirmation of a grade of being. This implicit affirmation of maximal being in every affirmation of a degree of being is simply the intellect affirming a degree of existing as a degree, by reason of the latter affirmation failing to satisfy the intellect tending or dynamically oriented to the infinite, as has been explained.

Perhaps Korinek's notion of indirect comparison may furnish another view of how absolute being grounds the similarity between different entitative acts. Might not the intellect, reflecting on the first step in the fourth way, consider that the proximate reason for the similarity between two different degrees of existing is that both the affirmation of an inferior degree of being and the affirmation of a superior degree of being fail to satisfy the natural appetite of the intellect? This dissatisfaction—intelligible only, as has been repeatedly emphasized—provided that the intellect strives to go beyond the act of affirming-not-satisfying-the-intellect to an act of affirming-completely-satisfying-the-intellect, namely, affirming the truth of attributing a predicate to the subject in the statement "There is Pure *Esse*," describes Korinek's theory of indirect comparison. And might not the intellect scrutinizing the second step in the fourth way recognize that the ultimate reason for the likeness between various grades of existing is that affirming the truth of the plenitude of being, which is imitated by all the degrees, completely satisfies the natural appetite of the intellect? Thus the outer approach to the absolute developed in the first part of this chapter goes hand in hand with the inner path to God described in Korinek's theory of indirect comparison. Stated in another way, different degrees of existence imitating absolute being is duplicated by the human intellect's affirmation of a degree of existing naturally tending to affirm the truth of the plentitude of being because being is intelligible.[14]

With this dual explanation the fourth way avoids begging the question.[15] Such a fallacy would be committed were explicit knowledge of maximal being claimed in the initial step of the fourth way. It is avoided, however, because the argument asserts only implicit knowledge of the supreme being in the first part of the demonstration.

In recapitulation of the contrasts between a grade of the act of existing and a part of quantity, six characteristics of the perfection of existing are specified by Korinek. The act of existing of a superior finite being does not result from adding together the acts of existing of two inferior beings, but is qualitatively better than the perfection of existing of a lower being, is a simple quality without parts and is called a degree of existing. Affirming the act of existing of a being of experience includes implicit knowledge of maximal being; the fourth way concludes to explicit knowledge of the truth of the illimited act of existing. In the first stage of the fourth way, affirming that different grades of existing are similar involves an indirect comparison of these degrees with maximal being implicitly affirmed in every affirmation of a degree of being.

An Objection

Although objections to understanding the fourth way are as numerous as the difficulties of walking through thorny underbrush, the final method of clarification used in this essay will propose only one objection because the two parts of Aquinas's text on the fourth proof provide the basis for a double answer to the difficulty. A student once expressed this same objection at the end of his seminar report on the proof of God from the degrees of perfection. "The failure of the fourth way," he commented, "to account for the essences of graded beings is the only difficulty preventing me from assigning certitude to the conclusion of the fourth way." As the first part of Thomas's text concerning the fourth argument has already been cited in this study, only the second part of this quotation is now reproduced.

> "Now that which is predicated maximally in a genus is the cause of all in that genus; e.g., fire, which is maximally hot, is the cause of all hot things, as is said in the same book. Hence there is a reality which is for all things the cause of their being, goodness and every other perfection; and this we call 'God'."[16]

How, then, does the bi-partite structure of the text about the fourth way dissolve the difficulty? The two parts of the passage correspond to the two stages in the resolution of the objection. The purpose of the first part of the text is to ascend from the affirmation of the degrees of existing to the affirmation that there is the maximal being, the exemplary cause of all graded beings. Since this procedure constitutes a proof (for God) whose scope is to explain the similarity of the different notes on the scale of existence in limited beings, failure to explain the essence of these beings is not a deficiency in the argument. This is the first stage of the reply to the difficulty previously proposed.

As L. Charlier[17] in his recent article on the five ways maintains that the second part of the text regarding the fourth way deals with the procession of creatures from God, the First Efficient Cause, his analysis of this part of the passage explicitly treats the origin of the essence of a limited being. Therefore, according to him, the intent of the second part of the text is to descend from affirming that there is the highest degree of being, the First Efficient Cause of the degrees, to affirming the degrees of being. How does he understand this efficient causality? It has three aspects. First of all, maximal being, the efficient cause, grounds the *similarity* between graded beings and itself. In the words of Aquinas,

> "For since every agent reproduces its like so far as it is an agent, and everything acts in accord with its form, the effect must in some way resemble the form of the agent. ...In this way all created things, so far as they are beings, are likened to God, as the first and universal Source of all existence."[18]

Secondly, the highest degree, efficient cause, guarantees the act of *existence* of graded beings. God's efficient causality must not be conceived quantitatively as if God loses parts of His own act of existing by placing particles of the act of existing "outside Himself" as creatures.[19] Rather, the highest degree of the act of existing is qualitatively "present to all the degrees by imparting itself to them without division or loss to itself."[20] When Robert Frost explained his poem "The Hired Man" to an audience of a thousand persons, he did not lose parts of his own knowledge by giving each member of the audience a particle of knowledge, as a waiter distributes after-dinner drinks. Rather, Frost's thought was qualitatively present to all the listeners by the entire discourse being spoken to all at the same time, without division of or loss to the speaker's knowledge. To express the communication of existence another way, limited being constantly borrows its being from God, surely distinct and not separated from the divine being, but totally dependent on infinite being, its source. Thirdly, the supreme being, efficient cause, establishes the *multiplicity* of the beings in the degrees. Multiple beings are each composed of intrinsic principles of being, essence and the act of existing, which are related as potency and act. The potential component, essence, which limits its correlative act of existing, accounts for the multiplicity of participated beings. God, the supreme principle of graded beings, creates the essence of such beings *with* the existence.

> "God at the same time gives *esse* and produces that which receives *esse*."[21]

This explanation of the origin of the essences of limited beings is the second stage of the response to the initial objection that the fourth way fails to take into account the essences of graded beings.

How the two parts of the text correlate with the two phases, in the dissolution of the difficulty first proposed, may now be summarized. Although the first part, which contains the fourth way, accounts not for the essences of limited beings but for the similarity between different degrees of entitative acts by affirming that there is the infinite act of existing, the second part, which identifies maximal being with the First Efficient Cause, implies that both the essence and the *esse* of limited beings take their origin from Pure *Esse*. Thus, it is true that the fourth way itself does not consider the essence of a limited being; but the second part of the text on the fourth proof does take up the essence of a limited being by implying that such an essence proceeds from Pure *Esse*.

Conclusion

Has this chapter succeeded in clarifying the fourth way? Comparing three recent interpretations of the fourth proof with the position presented in this essay may help answer this question. Although all four writers seek to ground the principle of exemplary causality, namely that different degrees of existing are affirmed insofar as they imitate differently the unlimited act of existing, they explain that ground differently. The first author[22] claims that the principle of exemplary causality is true because

> "the source of the intelligibility of these minorated degrees of the same perfection...[can be]...only the existence of the unlimited, unreceived degree."

The second philosopher[23] expresses the evidence for the principle of exemplarity as follows.

> "If that which is in the highest degree were not existing, if it were pure creation of my intellect, I would find myself with this inexplicable and contradictory fact:...a perfection which of itself does not admit limit and which does not exist in itself is found among things graded and limited."

The third writer[24] says the basis for the exemplary proposition is that

> "this absolute...[explains]...why one and the same value could be found more or less diminished in existents of lesser perfection."

This present essay grounds the exemplary causal proposition in this way. Affirming the truth of the plenitude of being, the exemplar, both being imitated differently by all the degrees of existing and completely satisfying the tendency of the intellect, ultimately accounts for the similarity between the different grades of existing. In view of these four explanations it does seem that this present quest has made the fourth way more understandable without claiming, of course, to solve completely the mystery of being.

The approach to God described in this study has other results. It reveals the total grandeur of finite beings mirroring, reflecting and imitating Pure *Esse*. It may serve as a philosophical basis for the poet's claim to find God in all things.

> "There was a time when meadow, grove and stream,
> The earth and every common sight,
> To me did seem
> Apparelled in celestial light."[25]

And it may provide a fundamental ingredient for a philosophy of society befitting the dignity of the human person in which priority is given to quality over quantity, to work over money, to the human over the technological, to wisdom over science, to the service of humanity over the unlimited aggrandizement of the individual or of the State.[26]

Footnotes to Chapter Two:

1. This manner of expressing a judgment of similarity between existents is taken from J. O'Brien, "Analogy and the Fourth Way," in *Wisdom in Depth*, ed. V. Daues (Milwaukee, 1965), p. 177.
2. Aristotle, *Meta.*, VII, 8, 1034a 5-8.
3. For more complete explanations of a real relation of quantity cf. G. Klubertanz, *Introduction to the Philosophy of Being*, 2nd ed. (New York, 1963), pp. 272-273, and L. Sweeney, *A Metaphysics of Authentic Existentialism* (Englewood Cliffs, 1965), pp. 190-201.
4. S. Thomas Aquinas, *Summa Theol.*, transl. J. Anderson (Englewood Cliffs, 1963), I, 2, 3 c.
5. *Capita quaedam praelectionum Theologiae Naturalis* (Romae, 1963-1964), pp. 319-363.
6. *Ibid.*, p. 337.
7. *Ibid.*, p. 361.
8. *Ibid.*, p. 338.
9. *Ibid.*, p. 338, 361.

10. Cf. E. Gilson, *The Christian Philosophy of St. Thomas Aquinas*, transl. L. Shook (New York, 1956), p. 44. Aquinas's "metaphysics of being as being 'consignifies' existence. It does not 'signify' it unless precisely it uses the second operation of the understanding and employs all the resources of the judgment."

11. Cf. S. Thomas Aquinas, *De Ver.*, transl. R. Schmidt (Chicago, 1954), XXII, 2 ad 2. "All cognitive beings also know God implicitly in any object of knowledge. Just as nothing has the note of appetibility except by a likeness to the first goodness, so nothing is knowable except by a likeness to the first truth."

12. Cf. A. Korinek, *op. cit.*, pp. 344, 359, 360. This line of reasoning is developed fully below, Chap. Three.

13. Cf. J. Collins, *God in Modern Philosophy* (Chicago, 1959), p. 399, and J. Maritain, *Approaches to God* (New York, 1954), p. 13.

14. Cf. G. Smith, *Natural Theology* (New York, 1966), p. 35.

15. Cf. A. Korinek, *op. cit.*, pp. 338, 359, 360.

16. S. Thomas Aquinas, *Summa Theol.*, transl. J. Anderson, *op. cit.*, I, 2,3 c.

17. "Les Cinq Voies de saint Thomas," in *L'Existence de Dieu*, 2nd ed. (Tournai, 1963), pp. 221-213.

18. S. Thomas Aquinas, *Summa Theol.*, transl. J. Anderson, *op. cit.*, I, 4,3 c.

19. Cf. A. Korinek, *Problema Creationis et Providentiae* (Romae, 1964), p. 56.

20. A. Boekraad, *Philosophy of God* (Loyola University, 1965), p. 57.

21. S. Thomas Aquinas, *De Pot.*, transl. L. Shapcote (Westminster, 1965), III, 1 ad 17.

22. M. Holloway, *An Introduction to Natural Theology* (New York, 1959), p. 127.

23. L. Charlier, *op. cit.*, p. 210.

24. F. Genuyt, *The Mystery of God*, transl. J. Pilch (New York, 1968), p. 44.

25. A. Huxley, *Ibid.*, p. 172.

26. J. Maritain, *Integral Humanism*, transl. J. Evans (New York, 1968), p. 207.

CHAPTER THREE

A FACT OF KNOWLEDGE AND GOD'S EXISTENCE

This discourse begins in wonder about a fact of knowledge, namely, my act of affirming that outside my window an apple tree, covered with white blossoms as if by a heavy snow, exists. Of course, my affirming activity is a relation with a subject and a term. Evidently the subject is myself. And the relation has the existing tree as its term. Just as the explorer, upon first discovering the Mississippi River, set out to find the source and the mouth of that stream, so I want to know the Ultimate Source of my own act of judging tree existence and the Last Term of that same judgmental activity. Hence there are two questions here. The first question is about efficient causality. In this question I am not asking if the First Cause of myself is absolute being. Rather I am inquiring whether the First Cause of my act of affirming a tree's existence is absolute existence. In Chapter One I have answered this inquiry regarding efficient causality in the affirmative. The second question concerns finality. At this point I am not seeking to know whether the Ultimate Term of a tree producing apples is infinite being. But I am wondering if the Last End of my act of judging a flowering tree's existence is the infinite existence. To answer this question about the finality of my intellectual activity is the ambition of this discussion.

The same question may be formulated more amply. Can my act of affirming the existence of a certain tree be the starting point for demonstrating the existence of the Ultimate End of that same affirming activity? In even more detail, does an analysis of the above affirming action reveal an intellectual characteristic which so guarantees the existence of a Last Term that the negation of God as the Ultimate Term of this trait introduces a contradiction into this mental aspect itself? To bring this contradiction sharply into focus is the intent of this investigation. We call this procedure a rational demonstration of God's existence.[1]

Why should there be another essay on the above topic at this time? Recent excellent, detailed versions of the argument for God's existence from the dynamism of the human intellect make one wonder whether a succinct presentation of this demonstration might be given. This essay is an attempt to articulate such a concise reasoning process.[2]

What method shall we employ to answer the central inquiry of this study? As an art historian, seeking the causes and effects of Raphael's masterpiece *School of Athens*, carefully questions each part of the painting,[3] so, in our quest of the absolute from our own affirmation that a flower-laden tree exists, we shall interrogate each aspect of that affirmation. Thus our mind's journey to the infinite from our starting point will consist of systematically questioning each facet of that tripartite initial step: our affirming activity, the subject affirming and the existing tree affirmed. To view our procedure from a different angle, we shall scrutinize not only our act of affirming but also this same act of judging both as it proceeds from the knower and especially as it terminates in a particular existent. But by no means in this study do we claim to give a comprehensive account of human affirmation.[4]

Affirming Activity

To begin with the affirming activity, a general question about that activity comes to mind. What kind of a judgment occurs when someone affirms that this blossom-laden tree exists? Surely anyone granting that a direct judgment is the affirmation of an object some of whose characteristics can be known by the external senses will answer that the judging activity in question here is direct judging. For at the same time that someone affirms the existence of the tree nearby, such an individual also sees the green color of the leaves and the height of the tree.

The definition of a direct judgment just given suggests a further question. Is direct affirming an act of intellection or an act of sensation? Indeed there is more to affirming that the tall tree exists than merely seeing the white color of an apple blossom on the tree. For one thing, a person's act of direct judging that such a tree exists is at the same time an inadvertent awareness of that direct judgment. This awareness is named reflexive knowledge in this essay. Such inadvertent awareness can be verified by asking two questions of a student who has just judged that this tree in bloom exists. "When you affirmed that this neighboring tree exists, were you also aware of this affirmation? While you were making this initial act of affirming were you deliberately aware of this act before you were asked about it?" Undoubtedly the first question would be answered affirmatively and the second question would receive a negative reply. On the other hand, an act of seeing the white color of an apple flower is not simultaneously reflexive knowledge. No one would claim seeing an act of seeing the white color of the blossoms on the tree. Hence an act of direct affirming is simultaneously reflexive knowing; this is not true of an act of sensation. Consequently direct judging is not sensation but a richer act of knowing than sensation. We entitle this richer cognitive activity intellection. From the difference just pointed out between direct affirmation and sensation it follows that, while seeing proceeds from the power of sight in the human knower, direct judging can never proceed only from a sense power but must follow from a human subject's reflexive faculty which we call the intellect.

Having established that affirming the existence of a campus tree is an act of direct intellectual judging proceeding from the intellect in a human person, we now ask about the very being of that affirming activity. What is the reality of the activity itself of judging that this tree with green leaves exists? All who consider their own act of affirming that this fruit-bearing tree is will admit that in this intellectual activity a knowing subject goes beyond itself to be united in some way with the affirmed tree. Now the unity in question here is either physical, specific, numerical or intentional. It is surely not physical unity, the unity resulting from substantial change, as occurs in the case of an apple eaten by a boy, because affirming the existence of the tree adorning the campus does not change the tree. Further, the unity under consideration is certainly not specific unity, the unity between two things belonging to the same species, since the person judging and the judged tree differ specifically. Nor is the judgmental unity numerical like the unity between the President of the United States and the person now holding that office. Obviously the subject affirming and the object affirmed here are not the same thing. Hence it remains that the unity of the act of affirming is intentional. By this we mean that when anyone affirms this living tree is, somehow the subject affirming is the tree affirmed in an intellectual way. That is to say, the activity of affirming is an intentional act of existing, an intentional *esse*. To sum up, the reality of the act of affirming a particular tree's existence is neither a physical unity, nor a specific unity, nor a numerical unity, but an intentional unity or an intentional *esse*.[5]

This view that an act of direct judging is an intentional act of existing leads to another question. What type of intellectual knowing process is employed in coming to affirm the intentional esse of directly judging that this tree is? Introspection, defined as a deliberate turning of the mind from its direct judgment to affirming an aspect of that direct affirming activity, seems most accurately to describe the mental action performed by an individual who begins affirming that a tree shading the campus exists and then discovers that this very act of affirming is an intentional esse. For all three features of introspection as just described—direct judging, deliberate turning from that judgment and knowing an aspect of that same judgment—are verified in our case of someone learning that direct affirming is an intentional act of existing. First, notice that even a person who has never considered philosophical questions, seeing a beautiful tree, would admit if asked that this object exists. In this way such a person directly judges. Secondly, only a subject willing to follow a sequence of questions and answers will turn from directly affirming a tree's existence to acknowledge that this direct judgmental act is an intentional esse. Of course such a willing transition from direct knowledge is deliberate. Thirdly and obviously, to assert that direct affirming is an intentional act of being is to know an aspect of that affirmation.[6] Briefly, the mental change from direct judgment to affirming the intentional existence of that judgment is introspection.

Comparing our introspective method with Kant's famous disjunction exhibits another facet of that method. Just as Copernicus, the astronomer, had said that either the stars revolve around the spectator or the spectator revolves around the stars, so Kant, the metaphysician, claimed that either the concept conforms to the object, or the object conforms to the concept.[7] For Kant there is simply no middle ground between these two extremes. But introspective cognition, such as knowing the activity of directly judging that a shade tree exists, provides an intermediary since by such introspection we know not a concept, nor an object of direct judging, but direct judgmental activity itself arising from a subject and terminating in an object.

At this point in our investigation we may express more

precisely the method to be used in the rest of this study. Henceforth under the light of our own introspective knowledge we shall conduct the questioning of our direct judging that a certain sensible object exists. An example of introspective knowing is not "I think this object is" but rather "I internally witness that I am thinking this object is." So important is introspection to the mind's way towards the absolute to be elaborated in our essay that this mental approach to the infinite, if separated from introspection, dies as surely as a plant uprooted from the soil. This method also has the advantage of appealing to those seeking a knowledge of the Ultimate End by introspecting their own internal experience.[8] Isn't this similar to St. Augustine's discovery that truth is an interior path to God? Therefore we invite the reader throughout the remainder of this study to follow our procedure by introspecting and analyzing his own or her own direct cognition.

The Affirming Subject

According to the method just described we here raise a question about the affirming subject. Take note that we cannot always be actually introspecting all that the affirming activity contains. And so we must be content with proceeding in an orderly fashion by taking up one element after another of that judgmental activity. Can I establish from introspecting my own internal act of directly judging the existence of a tree laden with apple blossoms that I, the affirming subject, exist?

Introspection of my own direct cognition affirming this fruit tree's existence discloses that I am the one who is performing the direct cognitive act. Expressed differently, in some sense I am the source of my own direct cognition; and this is not denied by any philosopher. Having already recognized that an act of direct intellection is an intentional esse, I can argue that either the *esse* of my direct affirming proceeds from myself as an existing source or it arises from myself as a non-existing principle. But the latter alternative is unintelligible. Being never comes from non-being, in the words of Parmenides, the father of metaphysics. It follows that the esse of my direct judging comes from myself as an active existing source. Hence my own introspective activity, with the help of some disjunctive reasoning, has justified my existence as an affirming subject.

But isn't this procedure the same as Descartes' celebrated formula "I think, therefore I am"? It seems not for at least two reasons. First, by thought Descartes understood not direct judgments about the existence of an external sensible object but rather understanding, willing, imagining and feeling.[9] Second, the father of modern philosophy never affirmed that thinking is an intentional act of existing. Clearly my inner way of knowing my own existential act differs from Descartes' method of grounding his own existence.

My Mind as Natural Desire

With the existence of the affirming subject established we next examine that subject's intellectual natural appetite, both a necessary thought characteristic and a key element in our demonstration of God's existence. Through introspecting my act of affirming the tree's existence am I conscious of my mind's natural appetite? If I am aware that I judge a tree is, then affirm this blue jay on the lawn exists and subsequently acknowledge the existence of a certain student in my office, I am conscious of movement in my mental activities. Consciousness of this intellectual motion leads me to conclude that this change has a source which I call my mind's natural appetite, the root principle of all my intellectual activities. Several years ago a college graduate who had received a fellowship from a prestigious university to do graduate work in a highly specialized field wrote to me. "I am not going to attend graduate school because after eight weeks spent in Europe I want to know more about history, literature, music, art and philosophy." This sentence describes the student's insatiable curiosity, her intellect's natural tendency to know. Then too, the opening sentence of Aristotle's *Metaphysics* is about this natural yearning of the mind. "All men by nature desire to know."[10] Thus examination of my many mental cognitive acts manifests that my mind's natural desire is the source of those activities.

This tendency may be viewed from another perspective through Jean Javaux' explanation of the mind's natural appetite. According to him a human person's powers of sight and of possible intellect can both be considered as natural desires, innate tendencies. My faculty of sight is both passive and active. A white object in front of me imprints in my power of seeing a sensible form which moves that faculty to see the white item. In its passive role my faculty of vision is a capacity for receiving a sensible form; in its active role this same faculty determined by the sense impression is the active potency by which I see the colored object. Therefore there is in my power of sight a passive and active orientation with all possible colored objects. Without this link the faculty would not be moved by a colored thing. We call this dynamic bond of sight with its object "natural appetite." Likewise my possible intellect is both passive and active. In the presence of an existing tree in full bloom with white flowers, the conjoined activities of my senses and my agent intellect imprint in my possible intellect an intelligible form which moves that power to understand the existing tree. As passive my possible intellect is a potency for receiving an intelligible form; as active this same power actuated by the intelligible impression is the active potency by which I understand the tree existent. Consequently there exists in my possible intellect an active potential correlation with all possible existents. Without this bond the intellectual knowing power would remain unaffected by a material existent. This moving link of the possible intellect with its object we name "natural appetite."[11] To summarize Javaux' analysis, my faculty of sight determined by a sensible species is a natural appetite seeking not merely an act of seeing, not only a colored thing, but rather an act of seeing a colored thing; my mind informed by an intelligible species is a natural appetite desiring not just an act of understanding, not solely an existent, but instead an act of understanding an existent. To state this another way, both sight and intellect are powers specified by operations which, in turn, are specified by objects.

Formal Object of the Desire

Having completed our analysis of a human mind's[12] natural appetite, the subjective pole of direct affirming activity, we turn our attention to the objective pole of this judgmental act, the formal object of that natural desire. By formal object we mean the aspect of an object that excites the interest of a certain active power or of a particular science in us.[13] By material object we signify in an object all the aspects which can attract the active powers or sciences in human beings. Let us consider the colorful tree mentioned earlier. If I am a geometrician my formal object will be the height and width of the beautiful tree. I can look on the fruit tree as a farmer and my formal object will be the quality of the fruit produced. If I am a painter my formal object will be the color, shadows and light of the living tree before me.

What is the formal object of my intellect's natural appetite? What aspect in every object understood stirs up the interest of my mind? Accordingly such an aspect necessarily is common to all the objects of my intellect's natural impulse. In my introspective activity doubling back on my direct affirmation about a particular tree's existence, I am conscious of two objects attained by my mental operations, an existing sensible tree perceived by direct affirmation and the esse of this direct judgment understood by introspection. What aspect common to both these objects interests my intellect? Two answers to this question are possible: material existents that can be known both by the senses and by the intellect and the immaterial act of existing that can be known only by the intellect. I discard the first reply because the sensible aspect of a material being is absent from the above object of introspection. On the other hand, intelligible existence is found both in the object of direct judging and in the object of introspective knowing. A boy drinking water knows his thirst is quenched both by water and other beverages. While I grant that a sensible existent is the proper formal object of the human intellect, i.e., the object attained by direct affirmation, I maintain that intelligible existence is the total formal object of the human intellect, namely, the aspect common to both the object of direct judging and the object of introspective cognition. Therefore the fundamental aspect in every material and immaterial reality that interests my mental natural appetite is intelligible existence, the total formal object of my intellect's natural desire.[14]

Affirmed Object as Transcended

At this juncture we take up the affirmed object as transcended, the other important element in our argument for God's existence. Does my intellect affirming an existing sensible tree tend beyond judging this particular existent towards knowing further objects? Clarification is paramount here. I am not asking if my mind's act of direct affirmation transcends this particular object known. I am endeavoring to learn if my intellect's active potentiality presently judging the existence of a tree producing blossoms is dynamically oriented beyond this known arboreal existent in search of knowing other objects? In order to answer this question, once more I humbly attend to what my introspection going in and out manifests about my own direct affirmation of a growing tree. If I internally notice that my act of affirming a luxuriant tree's existence is succeeded by my act of judging a meadowlark's being, I recognize the movement in my mental activities. Awareness of this mental motion leads me to conclude that I have mentally transcended the tree. Evidently the act itself of affirming tree being does not go beyond this affirmed object; it remains that the source of my affirming activity, my intellect's natural appetite judging tree existence, goes beyond knowing that particular object to affirm later on animal being.[15] This transcending dynamism of the human mind's natural appetite is an undeniable fact that anyone can experience internally. To summarize, scrutiny of my changing affirmations about material things brings me to acknowledge that my intellectual natural appetite judging a visible thing transcends knowing that sensible existent and rebounds towards knowing other objects.

Affirmed Object as Limited

Continuing the inward exploration of our direct affirmation that a tree covered with blossoms exists, we seek at this moment to find out whether introspection of this same direct knowledge divulges evidence about the presence of a limitation factor in the affirmed object. Truly, outside of introspective knowledge, we recognize that the very multiplicity of trees requires a limitation component in each tree. Accordingly, because an apple tree is distinct from an existing peach tree, the former tree does not contain the whole perfection of existing and hence is limited. But to be consistent we choose to employ the introspective technique on our own direct judgment about a blossoming tree's existence in our search for a sign of the object's intrinsic limitation. If I am conscious that I affirm existence of a tree outside my room, then judge that a blue jay is on the lawn, I have perceived that affirming the apple tree does not completely satisfy the tendency of my intellect. If it did, my intellect would not go beyond knowing the tree to affirm animal existence. Hence, through knowing the failure of my affirmation about a tree's existence to fulfill totally the dynamism of my intellect, I directly experience that the tree is limited. A tourist in the Prado Museum viewing successively El Greco's paintings *St. John the Evangelist* and *Christ Carrying the Cross* would certainly admit that the first picture does not completely satisfy his aesthetic taste. If it did the visitor would not pass by the first masterpiece to look at the second artistic work of El Greco. If asked, the viewer would surely grant that, since it fails to satisfy completely his taste for beauty, El Greco's portrait of *St. John the Evangelist* has limited aesthetic beauty. And so, considering that my successive affirmations about material beings do not satisfy completely the impulse of my mind reveals the limitation of these material things.

Demonstration: First Stage

These introspective analyses of my own mental activity enable me to point out the precise intellectual characteristic to be employed in the task of demonstrating God's existence. This mental trait is not that I directly affirm a specific tree's existence but rather that my intellect's natural appetite affirming a certain existent tends beyond knowing that being in search of judging further objects. Does the existence in my intellect of a natural desire going beyond an affirmed finite being in quest of knowing other beings require affirming that infinite being, the Last End of the desire, exists?

In order to answer clearly the above basic question we present our reply in two stages. The first stage makes use of the following disjunctive syllogism. Either the interest of my mind's natural desire transcending an affirmed tree existent seeking to know another being is totally satisfied by knowing non-being, or it is completely satiated by affirming another finite being, or it is entirely appeased by cognition of the totality of finite beings or it is altogether gratified by knowing that Pure *Esse* exists.[16] Granting that what fully satisfies

the above transcending desire is intelligible and admitting that the above disjunction lists all possible solutions, if the first three members of the disjunction are contradictory, judging that Unlimited *Esse* is will correctly answer the question.

We can easily understand the defect in asserting that an intellectual natural appetite going beyond a judged tree existent is totally satisfied by affirming non-being. For we have shown that every mental innate impulse is satisfied by knowing intelligible existence, the intellect's total formal object, not by judging non-being.

It is also unsatisfactory to assume that the mind's innate tendency transcending an acknowledged arboreal existent is completely satiated by knowing another limited being. We have previously explained that a finite existent is a being failing to satisfy completely my intellect.

Equally unacceptable is the view that the mind's innate desire going beyond an affirmed tree being is entirely appeased by cognition of the totality of finite beings. Consistent with the definition of a limited being just given, the totality of finite beings is simply the totality of existents failing to satisfy fully my mind.

Having rejected as unintelligible the first three members of the complete disjunction stated before and taking for granted that what fully satisfies my intellectual innate appetite going beyond an acknowledged tree being in its desire for knowledge is intelligible, we may conclude that affirming there is Pure *Esse* is the correct explanation. From this it follows that my intellect's natural desire transcending all affirmed finite beings in its search for knowledge is an effect depending on the influence of judging that there is an infinite being, the First Final Cause of my mental natural desire, the Ultimate Good of my intellect's innate appetite.

At what precise moment does the effect, my intellect's natural appetite tending beyond knowing all finite things, occur? My mind is not always seeking above cognition of all limited beings. When my intellect uninformed by an intelligible species is not affirming material existence, my mind's natural desire is not tending to go beyond knowledge of all finite existents. But at the moment when my intellect actuated by an intelligible species affirms the existence of a material thing, that mind's natural dynamism is unleashed so as to strive beyond knowing all limited existents. For only when my intellect actuated by an intelligible species affirms the esse of a material thing, its proper formal object, does my intellect's natural appetite, at this point merely partially satisfied by knowing finite existence, actively seek to transcend its cognition of all finite beings in its desire for completely satisfying knowledge. As long as he is receiving a signal the pilot landing a plane by instruments alone knows that the aircraft is on the correct course for arriving at the airport. Consequently, simultaneous with my intellect's judgment of a material existent is the desire of my mind to transcend knowing all limited beings. To indicate the progress of our argument thus far, verifying that my mind's natural appetite going beyond judging all finite beings in its tendency to know is fully satisfied by acknowledging there is an infinite being completes the initial stage of our demonstration.

Demonstration: Second Stage

Just because up to this point I have showed the dynamism of my intellect affirming a material existent to be completely satiated by cognition that there is an unlimited being, it does not yet follow that I know there is an infinite who actually exists. Perhaps the infinite being corresponding to the total impetus of my mind only exists conceptually. The question still remains whether this natural impulse implies that I know that there is an actually existing infinite. Is this teleological drive in vain, as Sartre and Camus claimed, or is it intelligible? To answer this crucial query we proceed to construct the second stage of our argument.[17]

Our strategy in this last stage consists in making evident that infinite being, the Ultimate Object agreeing perfectly with my intellect's natural desire to know, is both internally possible and externally possible. If this can be done we shall have proved that my mind's natural appetite to know there is an infinite being requires knowing there is an actually existing infinite. We must keep in mind that natural appetite is not the same as an elicited appetite. We can have an elicited appetite, free choice of an object that is intrinsically impossible, such as trying to solve a problem having no solution. Our contention is that a natural appetite, a necessary tendency, cannot be in vain.

First, the intentional esse of my act of affirming tree existence demands the internal possibility of infinite existence. By an intrinsically impossible object we mean a being supposedly integrating two incompatible perfections. Such would be a college student who spends all his waking hours outside class on extracurricular activities doing very well in his studies. However, the object towards which my transcending mental appetite ultimately tends cannot be intrinsically contradictory. For, if infinite existence is intrinsically impossible, a degree of existence is also internally contradictory. If the lake is salty, a drop of lake water is also salty. But by introspection I have internally experienced a degree of existing, the intentional esse of my direct judgment about tree being. Since it is false that the intentional existence of my direct judgment about tree existence is internally contradictory, it is false that infinite existence is intrinsically impossible. Likewise if it is not true that a drop of lake water is salty, it is not true that the lake water is salty. Thus in the panorama of being the intentional esse of my own direct judgment concerning an arboreal existent discloses the internal possibility of Pure *Esse*, just as the gradual brightness of the dawn indicates the possibility of the brilliant sun.

Second, infinite existence is also externally possible. By an externally impossible object we understand an item whose causes for existence do not exist. This would apply to electric lights in a house located in an area where there is no distribution of electricity. But infinite being is not externally contradictory because it does not depend on a cause in order to exist. If infinite existence depends on a cause for its existence, infinite being would lack a perfection found in its cause, namely, the perfection of originating existence. In this case knowing that there is such a counterfeit infinite existent would not completely satisfy the impulse of my intellect's natural appetite. But in the first stage of the argument I have already established that my knowing there is an infinite being does fully satiate my mind's natural impetus. Hence, since it is false that infinite being lacks any perfection, it is also false that infinite existence depends on a cause in order to exist. In summary, being independent of causes the infinite is simply not a being whose causes for existence are absent; in other words, infinite being is externally possible. And so, explaining that the infinite actually exists on account of its internal and external possibility concludes the second stage of our argument.

At this time the two stages in our demonstration can be joined together. My mind's natural appetite affirming tree existence and going beyond affirming all finite beings in its seeking to understand is completely satisfied not by knowing there is a conceptual existing infinite but rather by knowing there is an infinite who really exists due to its internal and external possibility. This is to say, through the argument I "do not know God by himself as one individual object alongside others," but I only know that there is an infinite actually existing term of my intellect's dynamism.[18]

If we look back on the two-stage introspective argument given previously we can distinguish the following steps on the path we have followed to the absolute. First step: I directly affirm that a tree by my window exists. Second step: My intellectual natural appetite affirming tree being goes beyond this judged finite being in its orientation to know other objects. Third step: My mental natural appetite judging a tree existent transcends knowing all finite things in its striving to know. Fourth step: The previous step is an effect depending on the influence of my act of knowing that there is an infinite being, the Last End of my intellectual appetite. Fifth step: The drive of my mind's active potentiality surpassing my cognition of all limited beings in search of knowing is saturated, completely fulfilled by the knowledge that there is an actually existing unlimited, the Last End.

An Objection

Contrary to the statement just made it seems that my mind's natural desire is not completely fulfilled by knowing that an actually existing infinite, the unlimited end, is, because even at the conclusion of the argument my intellect does not yet possess this Last End. For my intellectual natural appetite existing in my finite being is on a different level than the plenitude of being, the real term of my mind's natural desire. An unlimited being desired but not accessible is a contradiction.[19]

One end possessed can be spoken of as the thing itself, the objective end, and, as the attaining of that same thing, the subjective end.[20] In the case of an archeologist discovering some ancient coins after digging in Egyptian ruins, the end viewed as a thing would be the coins, while the end regarded as the attaining of that thing would be the scientist's action of picking up the coins and carefully putting them in his pocket. Applying this double description of the end to my intellect's natural transcending appetite finding the good desired, the end as thing is infinite being, the Ultimate Object of the appetite. The end as attaining that thing is my intellect's natural tendency surpassing knowledge of all limited things analogously knowing that there is an actually existing unlimited.[21] Anyone reading the double stage demonstration given above and pausing at the end of the first premise in the first stage would possess no analogous knowledge from the premise itself. If the same person using our introspective technique completely understood the rest of the two-stage argument, such an individual would possess an analogous knowledge of absolute being. For this same person, through knowing the First Final Cause's effect, the intellect's natural appetite surpassing cognition of all finite beings in its desire to know, not only concludes with the affirmation that there is an Ultimate Subjective End of this desire, i.e., knowing there is an actually existing absolute, but also recognizes that infinite existent and finite existent are similar and different. They are alike in existing; they differ because the infinite is not the finite. This is as far as philosophy can go in answering this objection. We leave to theology how we know God in Himself.

The foregoing reply to an objection indicates my intellect's double role in this demonstration. First, as a spiritual knowing power, it is the faculty by which I reason from an effect to God's existence. Second, as a natural appetite tending beyond knowing all finite existents, it is also the precise effect used in the argument. All this is possible, of course, because being spiritual my intellect introspects not only its own object and operations but also itself as a power.

A Comparison

If I compare my cognition of a tree existent, the proximate subjective end of my intellect's natural desire, with my knowledge that there is an infinite, the Ultimate Subjective End of that same appetite, additional information about the double stage demonstration presented above comes to light. Both affirmation of tree being and intellection that an infinite exists attract my mental impulse. But the former judgment not completely satisfying my mental innate desire is about a limited being while the latter knowledge completely exhausting my intellect's natural tendency is about an unlimited being. I directly affirm that a tree exists; at the conclusion of our dual-stage proof I do not directly affirm Pure Esse but I merely know that the proposition there is an infinite who actually exists is true because my intellectual natural desire tending to go beyond my cognition of all finite beings is an effect depending on its First Subjective End, my knowing there is an actually existing infinite.

At what moment in our demonstration do I implicitly know that the proposition infinite being is is true? Accompanying my affirmation concerning the existing tree is my mind's impulse to transcend knowing all limited things. At this point I do have implicit knowledge that there is an unlimited being. Just as through seeing an arrow passing through the air I implicitly know that there is a target to receive the arrow, so through the dynamism of my intellect I implicitly know there is an infinite being, the Ultimate Term of this tendency.

When do I have explicit knowledge that the proposition an actually existing absolute, the Ultimate Objective End of my intellectual appetite, is is true? As we have seen, simultaneous with my mind's affirmation of a tree existent is the tendency of my intellect to go beyond knowing all finite beings. At this time I do not as yet explicitly know that there is an infinite being. If while judging the esse of a tree I introspect that cognitive activity, applying to it the dual-stage argument given above, I explicitly know that in affirming tree being my intellect's tendency seeking beyond knowing all finite beings can only be fully explained by my knowledge that there is a First Objective End of that tendency, an actually existing absolute. I now have explicit knowledge that the statement an actually existing infinite is is true.

From these remarks about implicit and explicit knowledge it follows that our demonstration was not a transition from knowing my mind's finite dynamism to knowing that there is an infinite but rather a rendering explicit what I did not at first recognize: my awareness of my intellect's limited tendency also included knowledge about absolute being. For example, an untutored sightseer of Michael Angelo's Sistine Chapel painting *Creation of Adam* might at first notice that the masterpiece portrays the moulding of the human body and only later realize that this same work of art also symbolizes the creation of a human soul.

Conclusion

Have we succeeded in our aim of developing a succinct rational demonstration of God's existence from the finality of the human intellect? It seems so because a denial of infinite existence as the Last Objective End of my mind's natural tendency transcending my knowledge of all limited existents introduces a contradiction into that natural appetite itself. If to my mind's natural appetite tending beyond knowing all finite things in its desire to know there is an actually existing infinite I at the same time join a negation, there is no infinite existent, then my transcending desire to know, to be another intentionally, becomes a desire to know, to be nothing intentionally. But to know, to be nothing intentionally, is contradictory. Similarly, for a normal person to see in a room from which all light illuminating color has been removed is contradictory. In short, a denial of God's existence renders my mental natural appetite transcending knowing all finite beings in its desire to know contradictory. Thus our proof expresses that the existence of my insatiable desire to know is an opening to my knowing that God exists. In the language of philosophy, our demonstration shows that the existence of my thought demands as its Ultimate Objective End the existence of God. The following verses indicate the overture to the infinite that we have presented in this essay.

> "A man's reach must exceed his grasp.
> Or what's a heaven for."[22]

The three foregoing chapters may be epitomized in the following lapidary statements. *Cogito cogitationem meam; ergo Deus est. Cogito gradus existendi; ergo Deus est. Cogito mentem meam transcendentem; ergo Deus est.*[23]

Footnotes to Chapter Three:

1. For an approach to God with a similar starting point cf. the following books: J. DeFever, S.J., *La Preuve Reelle de Dieu* (Paris, 1953), pp. 7-144, and J. Javaux, *Une Affirmation Raisonnee de Dieu* (Paris, 1974), pp. 5-128.

2. These presentations are in two new books. J. Donceel, S.J., *The Searching Mind* (Notre Dame, 1979), pp. 55-92, and K. Rahner, S.J., *Foundations of Christian Faith*, transl. W.V. Dych (New York, 1978), pp. 44-89.

3. Our formulation of an art historian's function is based on the description of art history given by W. Fleming in his *Arts and Ideas* (New York, 1974), p. 6.

4. This article presupposes the entire knowledge theory of Thomistic philosophy as Marechal expounds it. Basically he holds that any finite person who is knowing intellectually is an entity moved by the natural appetite of that person's intellect, and that the "true," i.e., the existent presenting itself to the mind, is a good for this power. Cf. Javaux, *op. cit.*, p. 91.

5. This analysis is adapted from J. Maritain, *The Degrees of Knowledge*, transl. G. B. Phelan (New York, 1959), pp. 111-115.

6. Explicit reflection is the term used by Javaux to name cognition about direct affirmation. *Op. cit.*, p. 38.

7. I. Kant, *Critique of Pure Reason*, transl. N. Smith (New York, 1965), p. 22.

8. In his book, *The Openness of Being* (Philadelphia, 1971), p. 84, E. Mascall asserts that whoever takes up knowledge first and only then inquires about being practices the transcendental method.

9. R. Descartes, "Principles of Philosophy," in *The Philosophical Works of Descartes*, Vol. I, transl. E. Haldane and G. Ross (New York, 1955), Principle IX.

10. Aristotle, *Meta.*, transl. Richard McKeon (New York, 1951), I, 1, 980a.

11. This explanation of the human intellect as natural appetite is adapted from Javaux, *op. cit.*, pp. 83-84.

12. "Mind" and "intellect" as used throughout the remainder of this essay always refer to the possible intellect.

13. This definition of formal object is taken from Javaux, *op. cit.*, p. 84.

14. Cf. S. Thomas Aquinas, *Summa Theol.*, transl. Fathers of the English Dominican Province (New York, 1947), I, 82, 4, ad 1. "If we consider the will as regards the common nature of its object, which is good, and the intellect as a thing and a special power; then the intellect itself, and its act, and its object, which is truth, each of which is some species of good, are contained under the common notion of good."

15. In the *SGG*, transl. V. Bourke (Garden City, 1956), III, 50, S. Thomas Aquinas mentions the transcending action of the human intellect. "Furthermore, nothing finite can fully satisfy intellectual desire. This is shown from the fact that, whenever a finite object is presented, the intellect extends its interest to something more, so that, given any finite line, it strives to apprehend a longer one; and the same thing takes place in regard to numbers."

16. DeFever, *op. cit.*, p. 141, summarizes Marechal's four versions of the transcending experience. We here briefly indicate one of them. "Affirmation grasps the actual reality of the object only because it simultaneously attains the object as limiting its active capacity. In other words, it grasps the real finite object in virtue of its tendency to a superior and last end." Transl. J.M.B.

17. This exposition is adapted from Javaux, *op. cit.*, pp. 94-98.

18. Cf. Rahner, *op. cit.*, p. 64.

19. Cf. Javaux, *op. cit.*, p. 106.

20. Cf. S. Thomas Aquinas, *Summa Theol.*, I-II, 13, 4.

21. Our answer to this objection is adapted from Javaux, *op. cit.*, p. 97.

22. R. Browning, "Andrea del Sarto," in *Victorian and Later English Poets*, ed. J. Stephens et al. (New York, 1937), p. 338.

23. "I think my own act of thinking; therefore there is a God. I think the grades of existing; therefore there is a God. I think my own mind transcending; therefore there is a God."

CHAPTER FOUR

ST. AUGUSTINE'S THEORY OF SEMINAL REASONS

The Problem

The purpose of this treatise is to explain the role of seminal reasons in St. Augustine's metaphysics.[1] Augustine envisions the whole of reality as divided into three levels: God or eternal reasons, the spiritual creatures and the seminal reasons. God is at the apex of reality since He is unchangeable as regards time and place. Spiritual creatures are next in the hierarchy of being as they are immutable in place but mutable in time. The seminal reasons together with all bodies are on the lowest level of things because they can change both in time and in place.[2] The problem of the seminal reasons in this world view can be expressed in three questions. What is the relation between the eternal reasons and the seminal reasons? What kind of causality do the seminal reasons exert? How are these reasons related to other terms of Augustinian metaphysics such as form, number, measure, weight and order? This discourse, then, is about the metaphysics of Augustine.

The solution of this problem will be a twofold procedure. The first step will be to express Augustine's thought about the relation between the eternal reasons and the seminal reasons, the effects of the seminal reasons and the connection between these reasons and various terms. The second step will be an interpretation of Augustine's views on these three questions by comparing his theory with the exemplary cause and the four causes: efficient, final, formal and material.

In the history of thought Augustine did not originate the theory of seminal reasons. Various philosophers who lived before him were acquainted with the notion. The Greek Stoics, Marcus Aurelius, and Plotinus used the terms *logoi spermatikoi*, while Cicero and Seneca wrote about the *rationes*.

The Argument

Why does Augustine incorporate the seminal reasons into his theory of reality? In his *Literal Commentary on Genesis* he proposes the seminal reason theory in order to explain the repetition in the first two chapters of *The Book of Genesis*. According to the account in the first chapter God created the plants and the trees on the third day, the fishes and birds on the fifth day. It was on the sixth day that God brought the animals into being and created man, male and female. Again in the second chapter of *The Book of Genesis* we are told that God brought forth from the ground the trees, the birds and the animals. He made man from the slime of the earth and Eve out of one of Adam's ribs. Augustine is puzzled by these two accounts of creation. Why does Scripture say in the second chapter that God produced these living beings when Scripture has already related in the first chapter that God made these creatures? Augustine answers that the first chapter story of the creation of things that will be born means that during the first six days God placed in the elements the invisible seminal reasons of all the trees,[3] fishes, birds, animals[4] and human bodies[5] that would exist in the world. The second chapter account of the formation of these same beings describes how during the time that followed the first week God caused these seminal reasons to grow into visible developed beings. Thus Augustine solves the problem of the repetition at the beginning of *The Book of Genesis*.

Wondering how God created all things simultaneously[6] during the first six days while living beings are born and die during the course of centuries, Augustine turns to the seminal reason theory for the answer. Simultaneous creation of all things during the first six days signifies that, during the first week, God scatters in the elements the seminal causes of all living things like plant pollen in an August wind. Living beings are born during the passage of time because the seminal powers of these creatures develop into visible beings.[7]

In his famous book *On the Trinity* Augustine finds that the seminal reason theory is a convenient way of explaining how Pharaoh's magicians produced animals from a stick and how Jacob's sheep bore offspring with spotted fleece. When Moses pleaded with Pharaoh to allow the Jews to leave Egypt, Pharaoh asked for a sign. Following God's command, Aaron cast his rod on the ground, and it was suddenly changed into a serpent. Pharaoh then looked to his magicians who likewise threw their rods on the ground. They too were turned into serpents. Aaron's rod became a snake because God willed that the good angels, having more perfect perception, arrange the elements so that the seminal reason hidden in the rod would suddenly burst forth into a reptile. With God's permission the evil angels did the same for the rods of Pharaoh's magicians.[8] Laban gave Jacob all the spotted sheep and goats in the flocks. Jacob increased their number by placing sticks of white and green in water troughs. When the pregnant sheep drank water, they saw the colored rods and bore spotted offspring. This occurred because whatever the mothers of these animals looked at with pleasure was followed by the seminal reasons of the offspring in proportion as these hidden reasons were more tender and could more easily be formed.[9]

Keen observer of nature as he was, Augustine maintains that the seminal reason theory explains some natural phenomena. For it is due to the seedlike principles that the earth brings forth plants whose seed was not previously sown in the earth, and that many animals on land and sea come into being without any union of male and female. For example, from the seminal causes in the corrupt bodies of animals arise other animals and insects.[10] In the case of bees, they do not produce offspring by sexual union, but they pick up in their mouths the seeds that are placed over the earth.[11]

Nature

Now just what is the nature of the seminal reason? Is it a substance or any one of the nine accidents of Aristotle? Since Augustine does not write about the categories of Aristotle, the seminal principle is neither a substance nor any of the accidents. It is an invisible force (*vis*) belonging to the wet element. Perhaps Augustine came to this conclusion because he records that every earthly thing that is born, including animals, trees and plants at the beginning, are formed and nourished by liquid.[12] Other terms that are equivalent or partially equivalent to the seminal reason are reason (*ratio*), quality (*qualitas*), power (*virtus*), cause (*causa*), potentia (*potentia*), principle (*principium*), origin (*primordium*), seed (*semen*) and rule (*regula*).[13]

Subject

Next in order logically is the consideration of the subject of the seminal reason. During the first six days God placed the seminal reason of the plants, trees,[14] animals[15] and human bodies in the earth. The reasons of birds[16] and fish[17] He created in water. Augustine explains that water is the subject of the seminal reasons of birds because they can only fly in moist air. No one ever saw any birds flying at the top of Mount Olympus in Macedonia where the air is not moist.[18] After the first week the seminal reasons developed into the first plant, tree, fish, bird, animal and human body. At this point the developed beings were the subject of seminal causes in three ways. First, the visible living being possessed the hidden power from which it itself had evolved. Second, the observable creature produced visible seed which is composed of the latent seminal reasons of future beings and the visible matter of the seed. For example, an oak tree produced the acorn which held the invisible reason of another oak tree. Adam produced human seed which held the seminal reasons of Abel and all the human bodies that would ever exist except Eve and Christ. After conception Eve carried the seminal reason of Abel until he was born. Third, living bodies were the subject of seminal reasons of insects and other animals. Therefore, the subject of seminal reasons include the elements earth and water, the developed living being and the visible seed.[19]

Creation

It is Augustine's view that, through the eternal reasons,[20] God created all creatures during the first six days.[21] More precisely, God created each single creature through the proper eternal reason of that creature. For example, there is a certain reason for a man and a different reason for a horse.[22] The eternal reason is the model of the creature like the pattern of a box in the mind of the carpenter.[23] These creatures were made either as definitive forms[24] or as seminal reasons. A creature with a definitive form is one that was made as a developed being and does not undergo growth or change in time. Creatures with such a form include the angels, the day itself, the firmament, the four elements, the stars and the human soul. On the other hand, seminal reason creatures are hidden qualities or powers which were inserted in the elements during the first week. Plants, animals and the human body were fashioned as seminal reasons. God created both definitive forms and seminal reasons when He said, "Let this creature be made," or, "Let that creature be made." When He thus made them, God called to Himself the imperfection of the creature; and turning to God the unformed creature received a form. The result was that the now perfect creature imitated the form of the Word.[25] The imperfection of the creature did not precede form in time because God concreated both simultaneously. For example, a speaker simultaneously produces the sound and the words.[26]

In his account of the first week, Augustine mentions Christ and miracles. God through eternal reasons made seminal reasons for every human body except the body of Christ. There is no seminal reason for the human soul,[27] although Augustine examines such a possibility at great length.[28] When He created the seminal principles, God placed in all of them a certain necessity and a passive capacity for receiving divine intervention. This necessity simply consists in the fact that God arranged it so that creatures can develop from these seminal principles.[29] An example of passive capacity in a seminal reason would be God's creation of the seminal power of a grape with the passive capacity from which divine intervention could produce wine instantaneously.[30]

To the question of why God created the universe Augustine answers, "Because of His own goodness alone."[31]

Conservation and Development

Besides creating them, the divine reasons play a main role in the history of the seminal reasons. They keep the seminal causes in existence[32] and cause them to develop in the time following the first week.[33] For example, the all-powerful reasons cause the seminal powers of animals to effect the birth, growth and death of these living beings. And it is on account of these supreme principles that no new type of creature is made.[34]

The eternal reasons cause the seminal forces to produce both ordinary and extraordinary effects. The divine principles influence some seminal causes as active powers to develop in a natural way.[35] Thus God causes the occult powers of all human bodies except the hidden principles of Adam and Eve to produce bodies that grow in size. In the case of extraordinary occurrences the supreme reasons by divine intervention produce miraculous effects from the passive capacity of other seminal causes.[36]

Adam and Eve were made in a different manner from other human beings. Augustine's thought seems to be that God caused Adam's seminal reason as an active power to produce the adult body of Adam with no gradual increase in size.[37] He inclines to the view that no miraculous intervention occurred here.[38] However, in the case of Eve, her seminal virtue is a passive capacity from which divine intervention produced her body.[39]

Is God the term of all created activity? Augustine answers that God brings all things to Himself who is rest and pure joy.[40]

Effects

As active secondary powers with no corresponding natural passive power seminal reasons produce the following ordinary effects: birth, manner of formation[41] and gradual growth or increase in size.[42] It is due to the seminal origins that the living being develops into a certain type of creature[43] and not another type.[44] Accordingly, a grain of wheat does not produce beans, a bean plant does not become wheat, a cow does not generate a man, and a man does not give birth to a calf.[45] Also the seminal principles make a certain creature exist at a certain time in the future, provided, of course, that God foreknows that this being will exist at that time.[46] In addition they change adjacent earth and water which are like matter into these distinctive characteristics: position of the parts, size, color, outer covering and shape of the being.[47] Other effects include all those things by which the being acts in time, the power of generation, the natural motions, the acts of the being, all that the being produces,[48] decrease in size, death[49] and time of death. For example, the seminal reasons as proximate powers produce these effects in trees and birds. They change the surrounding earth and water into these characteristics of the tree: position of branches, size and color of the leaves, the shape and richness of the fruit and whatever the tree produces. In birds they cause the feathers, wings and the actual flight of the bird.[50] The seminal reasons of human bodies produce all human bodies except the body of Christ.[51]

When miracles or extraordinary events occur, the seminal reasons are passive capacities from which the divine intervention produces a miraculous effect.[52] As was seen previously, Eve's body was formed from a seminal reason in a miraculous way. Another miracle was the sudden change of water into wine.

Condition

Although God causes the seminal reason to unfold and the seminal principle itself is a proximate power of the effect, the seminal cause breaks forth into a living being at one time in history rather than another because developed things in creation act as conditions of this growth. Since seminal reasons of some plants and trees sprout only after rain has fallen and the soil has been cultivated, water and cultivation of the soil may act as conditions for the burgeoning of these seedlike principles.[53] Although the corruption of living bodies is the condition for the springing forth of some animal seminal forces, conception is the usual condition for the evolving of seminal reasons of both animals and human bodies.[54] This was not true, of course, of Adam and Eve; but in the case of Pharaoh's snakes the angels scattering the seminal reasons where the elements are properly mixed can act as conditions for the development of the reasons.[55] Regarding Jacob's sheep of various colors, conditions for the increase of the seminal reasons into colored sheep include both Jacob's placing the colored rods before the pregnant sheep and the resulting image of these rods in the soul of the sheep.[56]

Metaphysical Terms

The last part of the problem is to compare the seminal reasons with various metaphysical terms used by Augustine, such as form, number, measure, weight and order. Although throughout his writings on seminal reasons hints are made about this comparison, all the data necessary to study these terms are given at this point.

There are two kinds of form in Augustine's writings, the internal, definitive form and the external form. The internal, definitive form of a living being below man makes the being be what it is.[57] Moreover, it produces the soul[58] of these beings;[59] and without it the living being would be nothing.[60] God, of course, is the primary cause of this form. Its secondary causes include intrinsic, efficient causes and seminal reasons which make number in the seminal reason develop and produce form.[61] The external form of a living being below man, on the other hand, is the figure or shape of such creatures. Therefore God is the primary cause and the seminal reason is the secondary principle of this latter form.[62]

The number of a living being below man is an intrinsic principle which causes form.[63] And if one removes form and number from the being, the thing would be nothing. At creation God placed number in the seminal reason of visible living beings. But the hidden seminal reason is a secondary cause of the number's development.[64]

The measure or mode which is in all seminal reasons is an intrinsic principle that bounds, limits and terminates creatures.[65] It also makes a being have neither too much nor too little.[66] In addition it is the principle causing the living being to grow in a fixed way, to reproduce itself in a definite manner and to have certain aptitudes.[67] As with number God put measures or modes in the seminal reasons at creation. In turn the seminal principles are the proximate causes of the unfolding of these modes.[68]

Weight contained in all seminal reasons of living beings below man is another intrinsic principle. Augustine describes it as a force, or a power, of a thing that causes that being to seek its own proper place.[69] In another text, Augustine says that it is the love of a creature that gives a being an appetite for its own proper place or for rest and order.[70] Again, God bestowed weight in the seminal reason when He created the world. Then too, the seminal principles are the proximate powers of the evolution of this weight.[71]

The last term to be considered is that order which is found among the parts of living beings below man and among the members of the human body. Because of this order, each equal and unequal thing is in its proper place.[72] The order also gives harmony to the creature.[73] As one might suspect in Augustine's theocentric universe, God causes this order.[74] Besides, the seminal reason is the proximate cause of this order.[75]

General Theory of Reasons

A correct perspective of Augustine's tri-level metaphysics requires a more detailed description of the second level of being. The whole of reality, then, is explained according to the theory of reasons. God, or eternal reasons, is at the pinnacle of all things; spiritual creatures are just below God; and seminal reasons together with all bodies are at the base of reality. The eternal reasons, as has been explained, create and conserve all creatures who are on the second and on the lowest levels of reality. Besides, these reasons play a key role in the cognition and beatitude of men and angels, who are on the second level of being. A man possesses wisdom when his higher reason uses eternal reasons to judge corporeal things, while he has science whenever his lower reason deals with corporeal beings.[76] The blessed man is turned towards (*conversio*) these higher reasons in contrast to the bad man who is diverted (*aversio*) from them.[77] The eternal reasons imprint the laws of justice on the good man's heart like a ring which stamps the figure of the ring on the wax and still retains the figure. As a matter of fact the light of Truth even touches sinners at some time.[78] However, the angels know creatures because they see the eternal reasons of these creatures.[79] As with men, the blessed angels are illumined by the light of the divine reasons.[80]

Solution

Since all the pertinent texts have now been analyzed, the problem of this essay—the relation between the eternal reasons and the seminal reasons, the causality of the seminal powers and the relation between these forces and various terms[81]—can be solved. The solution will be an interpretation of Augustine's thought on these three points by comparing his theory with the exemplary cause and the four Aristotelian causes. There is no difficulty in using the exemplary cause because Augustine frequently speaks about creatures imitating the divine ideas. But there is a difficulty in applying the four-cause theory to causality in Augustine since he neither defines a cause nor does he define the four causes—efficient, final, material and formal—which Aristotle has in his *Metaphysics*.[82] According to Aristotle, the efficient cause of the statue of Socrates is the sculptor. Now the sculptor made the statue to earn some money, which is a final cause of the artist. The marble, or that out of which the statue is made, is the material cause of the art product, while the figure of Socrates, or that which is made, is like the formal cause of the statue. No attempt will be made to force Augustinian doctrine into the Aristotelian framework; but where these causes are employed their use will be defined strictly according to Augustine's meaning.

What, then, is the relation between eternal reasons and seminal reasons? God through the eternal reasons is the efficient, exemplary and final cause of the creation of the seminal reasons. As the efficient cause, God also places in the seminal reasons a certain necessity, number, measure, weight and a passive capacity for receiving divine intervention. There is no active power corresponding to this passive power in these seminal powers. God is the efficient cause because He creates the seminal reasons; and He is the exemplary cause, since He made the seminal reasons by calling imperfect matter to Himself and making the matter imitate His perfect form. We can say that He is the final cause of this creative activity since He creates these reasons because of His own Goodness.

Also, God is the efficient, exemplary and final cause of the conservation and development of the seminal reasons. As efficient cause, He makes the seminal principles continually exist and develop either in an ordinary process or in an extraordinary manner, as happens in the case of miracles. In this latter case, the eternal reasons by divine intervention produce miraculous effects from the passive capacity of the seminal causes. He is the exemplary cause because He continually forms these powers by making imperfect matter imitate His infinite form. And lastly, He is the final cause here because He moves the seminal reasons towards Himself who is true rest and joy.

What is the causality of the seminal reason? It is a sort of secondary efficient cause of the development of the living being below man and of the body of man. The seminal reason is an invisible power, virtue or force, which exists in the elements, the visible seed, or in the developed being. As efficient cause or active power with no corresponding natural passive power, it produces the following natural effects: the birth, the manner of formation, the nature and the fact that it is the kind of being that it is, the existence of the being, the gradual growth or increase in size, the position of the parts, size, color, outer covering and the shape of the being. Other effects include all those things by which the being acts in time, the power of generation, the acts of the being, all that the being produces, decrease in size, death and time of death. When miracles occur, the seminal reason is a passive capacity from which divine intervention produces extraordinary effects.

Also the seminal reason resembles secondary final and formal causes. It is a final cause because it determines the above effects as that towards which the living being tends in its development. Lastly, it is a sort of formal cause because in living beings below man it causes number to develop and to produce the internal, definitive form.

However the seminal reason does not seem to be an exemplary cause; for in the writings of Augustine which we examined he does not say that the seminal reason bestows a form on anything by making that being imitate it. And it is not a material cause, because it does not appear that the seminal reason is matter out of which a certain living being is made.

The bodies of all men with the exception of Christ have a seminal reason. However, Adam and Eve seem to have been made in a different manner from other human beings. God caused Adam's seminal reason as an active power to produce the adult body of Adam with no gradual increase in size. In the case of Eve her seminal reason is a passive capacity from which divine intervention produced her body.

What is the relation between seminal reasons and various metaphysical terms? As secondary efficient, final and formal causes the seminal reasons effect the internal order, the external form, the development of number, measure and weight which these reasons contain. In living beings below man they cause number to develop and produce the internal, definitive form.

Augustine's theory of seminal reasons, then, is an explanation which maintains the supreme dominion of God, affirms the secondary causality of some creatures and asserts the unfolding of visible living beings. This account is quite different from emergent evolutionism such as many American naturalists maintain; but that is outside the scope of this study.

Appraisal

In evaluating Augustine's theory of seminal reasons three difficulties of this doctrine come to mind. First of all, seminal reasons explain the coming into being and the continued existence of living things below man and the body of man, but they do not account for change in the inorganic world. In fact, Augustine does not have any explanation of change in the realm of the non-living beings. Secondly, it would seem that Augustine says that nothing new substantially comes into the universe after the first six days. Then one must say that all changes in the world are accidental. It also follows that if there is only accidental change in the world, all created individuals are always of the same number and are always actually in existence. Besides, it would mean that when ten men eat a cow, the seminal reason of the cow continues to exist. It is hard to reconcile these conclusions with observable facts. Thirdly, Augustine says that the seminal reasons account for several facts: that some plants grow up without any seed having been planted and that bees gather the seeds of their young from the surface of the earth. However these incorrect observations of fact do not spoil the theory as a whole.

The theory of seminal reasons is also deficient because Augustine does not relate this doctrine with other aspects of his thought. He does not show the relation between the seminal reason of the human body and free, human acts. Moreover, he does not say whether or not the seminal reason of the human body plays any role in the transmission of original sin. Finally one would expect the theory of seminal reasons to play a part in Augustine's philosophy of history. However, he does not seem to relate the seminal reasons theory with the philosophy of history.

Conclusion

Studying Augustine's seminal reason theory through the screen of Aristotle's four causes and the exemplary cause has revealed that the seminal reason in a present living material thing is a hidden intermediary between God and the visible characteristics of that living being. From the viewpoint of God, the First Efficient, Final and Exemplary Cause influences the creation, conservation and development of the seminal reason. From the viewpoint of observable features, the seminal reason itself is a secondary efficient cause of the sensible aspects of a living thing, such as the leaves and fruit on a tree, the color and shape of a leopard, the height and the ambulations of a human person. Augustine, unacquainted with Aristotle's four causes, would have surely recognized God's presence in each living material thing as Creating, Conserving and Moving the living being's seminal reason to produce its visible effects.

Footnotes to Chapter Four:

1. Good secondary studies on the seminal reasons include the following: C. Boyer, *L'Idee de verite dans la philosophie de saint Augustin* (Paris: Beauchesne, 1920), pp. 97-137; E. Gilson, *The Christian Philosophy of St. Augustine,* transl. L. E. M. Lynch (New York: Random House, 1960), pp. 197-209; J. Martin, *Saint Augustin* (Paris: Alcan, 1923), pp. 311-314; M. McKeough, *The Meaning of the Rationes Seminales in St. Augustine* (Washington: Catholic University, 1926), pp. 28-96; C. O'Toole, *The Philosophy of Creation in the Writings of St. Augustine* (Washington: Catholic University, 1944), pp. 84-101; E. Portalie, *A Guide to the Thought of Saint Augustine*, transl. Ralph J. Bastian (Chicago: Henry Regnery Company, 1960), pp. 136-151. Father Woods's book is a fairly accurate treatment of the subject. H. Woods, *Augustine and Evolution* (Universal Knowledge Foundation, 1924), pp. 49-100. Dorlodot's work must be used with caution. For he wrote this book in order to see how much evolutionary interpretation Scripture would allow. He cited texts from St. Augustine which would confirm his position. C. Dorlodot, *Darwinism and Catholic Thought*, transl. Ernest Messenger (London: Burns Oates and Washbourne Ltd., 1922), pp. 1-130.

2. S. Aurelii Augustini, *De Genesi ad Litteram* (''Patrologiae Latinae''; Paris: Migne, 1844-1866), Bk. VIII, chap. 20, Vol. 34, col. 388. Further footnotes from this Migne series will list the abbreviated name of the work, the book and chapter numbers. Then the Migne series will be indicated by the letters PL which will be followed by the number of the volume and the column number.

3. *Ibid.*, VIII, 3; PL 34, 374-375.
4. *Ibid.*, IX, 1; PL 34, 393.
5. *Ibid.*, VI, 7; PL 34, 343-344.
6. Eccli. 18: 1.
7. *De Gen. ad Litt.*, V, 23; PL 34, 338.
8. *De Trin.*, III, 9; PL 42, 878.
9. *Ibid.*, III, 8; PL 42, 877.
10. *De Gen. ad Litt.*, III, 14; PL 34, 289.
11. *De Trin.*, III, 8; PL 42, 876.
12. *De Gen. c. Man.*, I, 7; PL 34, 179.
13. J. Brady, *Function of Seminal Reasons in St. Augustine's Theory of Reality* (St. Louis: Graduate School of St. Louis University, 1949), p. 250.
14. *De Gen. ad Litt.*, V, 5; PL 34, 326.
15. *De Gen. ad Litt.*, V, 5; PL 34, 393.
16. *Ibid.*, IV, 33; PL 34, 318.
17. *Ibid.*, V, 5; PL 34, 326.

18. *De Gen. c. Man.*, I, 15; PL 34, 184.
19. *De Gen. ad Litt.*, VI, 10; PL 34, 346.
20. *Ibid.*, I, 18; PL 34, 260.
21. *Ibid.*, IV, 34; PL 34, 319.
22. *De Div. Quaest.* LXXXIII, XLVI, 2; PL 40, 30.
23. *In Joann. Evang.*, I, 17; PL 35, 1387-1388.
24. Gilson, *op. cit.*, p. 206.
25. *De Gen. ad Litt.*, I, 4; PL 34, 249. "...ut in eo quod Scriptura narrat, 'Dixit Deus, Fiat,' intelligamus Dei dictum incorporeum in natura Verbi ejus coaeterni revocantis ad se imperfectionem creaturae, ut not sit informis, sed formetur secundum singula quae per ordinem exsequitur? In qua conversione et formatione, quia pro suo modo imitatur Deum Verbum, hoc est Dei Filium semper Patri cohaerentem, plena similitudine et essentia pari, qua ipse et Pater unum sunt (Joan. X, 30); non autem imitatur hanc Verbi formam, si aversa a Creatore, informis et imperfecta remaneat: propterea Filii commemoratio non ita fit quia Verbum, sed tantum quia principium est, cum dicitur, 'In principio fecit Deus coelum et terram;' exordium quippe creaturae insinuatur adhuc in informitate imperfectionis: fit autem Filii commemoratio, quod etiam Verbum est, eo quod scriptum est, 'Dixit Deus, Fiat;' ut per id quod principium est, insinuet exordium creaturae existentis ab illo adhuc imperfectae; per id autem quod Verbum est, insinuet perfectionem creaturae revocatae ad eum, ut formaretur inhaerendo Creatori, et pro suo genere imitando formam sempiterne atque incommutabiliter inhaerentem Patri, a quo statim hoc est quod ille."
26. *Ibid.*, I, 15; PL 34, 257.
27. *Ibid.*, VII, 26; PL 34, 368.
28. *De Lib. Arb.*, III, 21; PL 32, 1299-1300.
29. *De Gen. ad Litt.*, VI, 18; PL 34, 351.
30. *Ibid.*, VI, 14; PL 34, 349.
31. *De Civ. Dei*, XI, 24; PL 41, 338.
32. *De Div. Quaest.* LXXXIII, XLVI, 2; PL 40, 30.
33. *De Gen. ad Litt.*, V, 4; PL 34, 325.
34. *Ibid.*, IX, 17; PL 34, 406.
35. *Ibid.*
36. *Ibid.*, VI, 14; PL 34, 349.
37. *Ibid.*
38. *Ibid.*, VI, 15; PL 34, 349-350.
39. *Ibid.*, IX, 18; PL 34, 406-407.
40. *Ibid.*, IV, 4; PL 34, 300.
41. *Ibid.*, VI, 15; PL 34, 349-350.
42. *Ibid.*, V, 5; PL 34, 326.
43. Text proves Augustine does not hold transformism.

44. Many studies have been written on St. Augustine and evolution. Three different views on this subject will be given and appraised. Dorlodot, *op. cit.*, pp. 4, 82, says that St. Augustine "attributes the first origin of living beings to a natural evolution of inorganic matter, which became organized and ultimately living matter by the simple action of forces, or better still, of powers inherent in matter." This is not correct. Woods, *op. cit.*, p. 4, maintains that "St. Augustine's doctrine so understood has nothing that in any way favors Evolution." This is also false. McKeough, *op. cit.*, pp. 109-110, holds that Augustine's "doctrine of the gradual appearance of living beings upon the earth through the operation of natural laws and secondary causes, constitutes a satisfactory philosophical basis for evolution, and merits for him the title of Father of Evolution." This is the true interpretation.

45. *De Gen. ad Litt.*, IX, 17; PL 34, 406. "Omnis iste naturae usitatissimus cursus habet quasdam naturales leges suas, secundum quas et spiritus vitae, qui creatura est, habet quosdam appetitus suos determinatos quodammodo, quos etiam mala voluntas non possit excedere. Et elementa mundi hujus corporei habent definitam vim qualitatemque suam, quid unumquodque valeat vel non valeat, quid de quo fieri possit vel non possit. Ex his velut primordiis rerum, omnia quae gignuntur, suo quoque tempore exortus processusque sumunt, finesque et decessiones sui cujusque generis. Unde fit ut de grano tritici non nascatur faba, vel de faba triticum, vel de pecore homo, vel de homine pecus. Super hunc autem motum cursumque rerum naturalem, potestas Creatoris habet apud se posse de his omnibus facere aliud, quam eorum quasi seminales rationes habent, non tamen id quod non in eis posuit ut de his fieri vel ab ipso possit. Neque enim potentia temeraria, sed sapientiae virtute omnipotens est; et hoc de unaquaque re in tempore suo facit, quod ante in ea fecit ut possit."

46. *Ibid.*, VI, 17; PL 34, 351.

47. *Ibid.*, V, 23; PL 34, 337-338. "...Surrexit enim a radice, quam terrae primum germen infixit; atque inde omnia illa formata et distincta creverunt. Porro illud germen ex semine; in semine ergo illa omnia fuerunt primitus, non mole corporeae magnitudinis, sed vi potentiaque causali. Nam illa magnitudo, copia terrae humorisque congesta est. Sed illa in exiguo grano mirabilior praestantiorque vis est, qua valuit adjacens humor commixtus terrae tamquam materies verti in ligni illius qualitatem, in ramorum diffusionem, in foliorum viriditatem ac figuram, in fructuum formas et opulentiam, omniumque ordinatissimam distinctionem. Quid enim ex arbore illa surgit aut pendet, quod non ex quodam occulto thesauro seminis illius extractum atque depromptum est?"

48. *Ibid.*

49. See *supra* n. 45.

50. *Ibid.*, IV, 33; PL 34, 318. "Deinde quot diebus opus erat, ut aves

volarent, si a suis primordiis existentes, ad plumas et pennas per naturae suae numeros pervenerunt?"

51. *Ibid.*, X, 20; PL 34, 424.

52. *Ibid.*, VI, 14; PL 34, 349.

53. *Ibid.*, V, 6; PL 34, 327.

54. *Ibid.*, X, 20; PL 34, 424.

55. *De Trin.*, III, 8; PL 42, 876.

56. *Ibid.*, III, 8; PL 42, 877.

57. *De Civ. Dei*, VIII, 6; PL 41, 231.

58. *Ibid.*, XII, 25; PL 41, 374.

59. *De Lib. Arb.*, III, 21; PL 32, 1299-1300. In this book which was written early in his intellectual career, St. Augustine lists the four theories which may account for the origin of the human soul. He does not say that any one of the four theories is the correct solution because Scripture and the early teachers of the Church did not decide which of the four theories is the true explanation. The first opinion is that God creates the first soul which propagates the souls of all men. According to the second theory God creates a soul for each man that is born. In the third position God places the souls existing already somewhere else in the human body. The fourth solution is that already existing souls are joined to the human body of their own accord. In the *Literal Commentary on the Genesis* Augustine seems to say that Adam's soul joined his body of its own accord. In his work *On the Soul* written towards the end of his life Augustine says that he does not know which of the four theories is the correct solution to the problem of the origin of the human soul. *De Anima et ejus Origine*, I, 25; PL 44, 487-488.

60. *De Lib. Arb.*, II, 16; PL 32, 1264.

61. *De Trin.*, III, 9; PL 42, 877-878. "Ista quippe originaliter ac primordialiter in quadam textura elementorum cuncta jam creata sunt; sed acceptis opportunitatibus prodeunt. Nam sicut matres gravidae sunt fetibus, sic ipse mundum gravidus est causis nascentium: quae in illo non creantur, nisi ab illa summa essentia, ubi nec oritur, nec moritur aliquid, nec incipit esse, nec desinit. Adhibere autem forinsecus accedentes causas, quae tametsi non sunt naturales, tamen secundum naturam adhibentur, ut ea quae secreto naturae sinu abdita continentur, erumpant et foris creentur quodam modo explicando mensuras et numeros et pondera sua quae in occulto acceperunt ab illo, qui omnia in mensura et numero et pondere disposuit (*Sap.*, XI, 12) ..."

62. *De Civ. Dei*, XXII, 14; PL 41, 789. "Ipse namque operatione, qua nunc usque operatur, facit ut numeros suos explicent semina, et a quibusdam latentibus atque invisibilibus involucris in formas visibiles hujus quod aspicimus decoris evolvant."

63. *De Gen. ad Litt.*, IV, 3; PL 34, 299. "...numerus omni rei speciem praebet..."

64. See *supra* n. 61.

65. *De Gen. ad Litt.*, IV, 3; PL 34, 299.

66. *De Beata Vita*, IV, 32; PL 32, 975.

67. *De Gen. ad Litt.*, IX, 17; PL 34, 406.

68. See *supra* n. 61.

69. *Enar. in Psal.*, XXIX; PL 36, 222.

70. *De Gen. ad Litt.*, IV, 18; PL 34, 309.

71. See *supra* n. 61.

72. *De Civ. Dei*, XIX, 13; PL 41, 640-641.

73. *De Mor. Man.*, II, 6; PL 32, 1348.

74. *Conf.*, VII, 5; PL 32, 736-737.

75. See *supra* n. 47.

76. *De Trin.*, XII, 12; PL 42, 1007.

77. *Epist.* 18; PL 33, 85.

78. *De Trin.*, XIV, 15; PL 42, 1052.

79. *De Civ. Dei*, XI, 29; PL 41, 343.

80. *De Trin.*, XII, 15; PL 42, 1011.

81. To my knowledge, there is no secondary study of the seminal reasons in St. Augustine's writings which takes this approach to the subject.

82. Aristotle, *Meta.*, V, c. 2, 1013 A25-35.

EPILOGUE: PARTICIPATION

Anyone comprehending the preceding chapters should find it easy to understand various ways of expressing the fourth way participation theory. In striking language the late Rev. Gerald Phelan used to tell his students that God is Phelan in the sense that whatever perfection of existence Phelan has, God "already" is; moreover, he taught that Phelan is not God because whatever of limitation or essence there be in Phelan, God is not.[1] Describing participation concretely Rev. Romano Guardini wrote that each material thing is simultaneously a mirror reflecting divine perfection to us and a veil hiding God from us.[2] For Rev. A. Sertillanges participation meant that Divine *Esse* is at the top of the tower of all limited beings and yet circulates in all of them as their support and last explanation.[3] Suggesting participation St. Anselm said to God: "You are within me and around me, and yet I do not sense You."[4] To put participation metaphysically, in God *Esse* is Unparticipated because Divine Essence is *Esse*; in a finite being *esse* is participated since finite essence participates or limits esse. By way of summing up participation, on the one hand, as the principle of all other things, God is constantly present within all finite beings; and, on the other hand, as Something Existing above all contingent things and distinct from them, God transcends all limited beings.[5]

Therefore the Supreme Being in St. Thomas's fourth way is the God not of Deism but of Theism. In Deism, God is completely separated from the world He has freely created. But in Theism, God, not a particular being alongside of other particular beings, both transcends and is immanent to the world He continually keeps in existence. Otherwise expressed, not only does God transcend all human experience as Kant correctly noted, but also the Absolute is immanent in all things as Hegel accurately wrote.[6] One can't help wondering whether man's forgetfulness of God's presence in all human beings accounts for the current increase in disrespect for human life.

Footnotes to Epilogue:

1. F. Wilhelmsen, "The Christian Understanding of Being: A Thomistic Reading," in *The Intercollegiate Review*, Winter—Spring (1978), p. 93.
2. R. Guardini, *The Living God* (Chicago, 1966), p. 90.
3. A Sertillanges, *Les Sources de La Croyance en Dieu* (Paris, 1928), p. 429.
4. S. Anselm, *Proslogion*, ch. 16.
5. St. Thomas Aquinas, *Summa Theol.*, transl. T., Gilby (Garden City, 1969), I, 13, 8, ad 2.
6. E. Harris, "Atheism and Theism," in *Tulane Studies in Philosophy*, Volume XXVI (1977), p. 100.